MICHAEL TRENT

Legends of the Lawless: Pirates Vol. 1

500 BC – 1600 CE

Contents

Introduction

Throughout history's pages, the sagas of pirates have consistently enraptured the imagination. These sea raiders, often embellished in books and movies, have come to symbolize rebellion, adventure, and a quest for freedom. While much attention is given to the flamboyant pirates of the 17th and 18th centuries during the so-called Golden Age of Piracy, it's important to remember that piracy's roots stretch far deeper into the past, into an age when the oceans of the world were shrouded in mystery and fraught with danger. This book ventures into the lesser-known history of pre-1600 piracy, revealing tales of audacious journeys, fierce combats, and the relentless pursuit of treasure and liberty.

Envision the world as it was before 1600: a place where maps ended in blank spaces and mysterious legends, where the phrase "Here be dragons" marked the unknown perils of the vast oceans. During this epoch, seafaring was not only an endeavor of exploration but also a battle for survival against the merciless elements of the sea. Into this daunting world sailed the early pirates, who were not mere outlaws and looters but often pioneers venturing into the unknown margins of the world.

These early pirates defy the stereotypical images of flag-bearing, parrot-accompanied figures of pop culture. They were a diverse group with varied backgrounds, motivations, and tactics. Some were rogue sailors, disenchanted with the growing control of emerging nation-states over the seas. Others were revolutionaries and exiles, seeking fortunes and recognition far from the constrictive societies of their homelands.

The tale of piracy before 1600 is also one of pioneering in naval technology and tactics. These early pirates were among the initial masters of naval combat, utilizing smaller, more agile ships to outsmart the bulky vessels of state navies. They forged strategies that would be emulated by both pirates and navies for centuries to follow. Their actions transcended simple acts of plunder; they were often elaborate operations requiring deep strategic planning and extensive maritime knowledge.

This period was also marked by significant cultural interactions and conflicts. Pirates often became intermediaries between diverse worlds out of necessity. They connected distant lands in ways no one else did at the time, merging different goods, ideas, and cultures. In their lawless existence, they forged a unique culture, an amalgamation of various maritime traditions that influenced life both at sea and on land.

Yet, the life of a pirate was far from a tale of unrestrained freedom. It was a hazardous existence, characterized by violence, treachery, and often a tragic end. The stories of these pirates are filled with fierce battles, mutinies, and desperate bids for survival. They dwelled in the shadows, perpetually fleeing from the naval forces tasked with their capture. Their final moments, whether in combat or at the executioner's noose, were as varied and dramatic as their lives.

Embarking on this journey through the untold tales of pre-1600 pirates is not merely an exploration of the past. It is the rediscovery of a neglected chapter in the history of the world's oceans. These stories provide a glimpse into an era where the sea was a realm of both potential and danger, and the line between hero and villain was often indistinct.

In this book, we sail side by side with these legendary figures, sharing in their victories and defeats. We will trace the origins of piracy back to ancient times and follow its development through the Middle Ages. We will encounter figures lost in the shadows of history, eclipsed by their more notorious successors. Through their experiences, we see a world where the horizon was just the beginning, and what lay beyond was a realm of the unknown.

As you turn these pages, prepare to be transported into a world starkly different from our own, yet one that has significantly influenced modern maritime law, international relations, and our perceptions of rebellion and autonomy. Each chapter will peel back the layers of myth and reality, presenting these pirates not simply as criminals of the high seas, but as intricate characters molded by their unique circumstances and era.

Teuta

I llyrian Queen Teuta stands out as a remarkable and influential figure in the rich tapestry of Illyrian antiquity, embodying the spirit and heritage of ancient Albania. Her legacy, intertwined with the mystique of the pirate queen, is enshrined in folklore that celebrates her extraordinary wisdom, unparalleled bravery, and ethereal beauty, often comparing her to the cunning of a snake, the courage of a lion, and the allure of fairies.

The realm of Illyria, where Queen Teuta's story unfolds, was a region of immense geographical and cultural diversity. It stretched along the Adriatic Sea to the west, reaching the flowing waters of the Morava River to the east. This historic land is now shared by several modern nations, including Croatia, Bosnia and Herzegovina, Slovenia, Montenegro, Kosovo, Serbia, and Albania, each inheriting a part of Illyria's rich legacy.

Born around 268 BC into a noble family, Teuta was not only the first child but also a trailblazer in her own right. She grew up receiving a traditional education, but her upbringing was marked by an exceptional element - she was trained in the ways often reserved for boys. This unique aspect of her early life included mastering the art of war, excelling in hunting, and becoming an adept horse rider, skills that would later define her reign.

The Illyrians, much like their Spartan contemporaries, held a progressive view regarding the role of women in society, particularly in martial affairs. Women were encouraged to learn combat skills and participate in warfare. Teuta, with her rare beauty and formidable skills, captivated the heir to the Illyrian throne, who chose her as his queen.

Her marriage to King Agron was not just a union of hearts but also a partnership in ruling a kingdom. Teuta was first and foremost a warrior queen - aggressive, hotheaded, and fiercely just. Their marriage, which lasted 18 years, was a golden era for the Illyrian kingdom, marked by significant strides in politics, economy, and military prowess.

The year 231 BC marked a turning point in Teuta's life. Following King Agron's death, she ascended the throne and ruled in the name of her young stepson, Pinnes. Under her leadership, the mighty Illyrian state expanded its territories, stretching from the left bank of the Neretva river to Epirus and encompassing numerous islands, with the notable exception of Vis.

In the brief yet transformative period following her ascent to the throne, Queen Teuta of Illyria demonstrated an extraordinary capacity for leadership and strategic acumen. She not only fortified her position of power but also forged formidable alliances that extended her influence far beyond her immediate realm. Her reign was characterized by a series of bold reforms, many of which built upon the foundations laid by her late husband.

One of Teuta's most significant achievements was the stimulation and revitalization of the Illyrian economy. She undertook initiatives that promoted the growth and development of Illyrian cities, turning them into bustling centers of trade and culture. Under her guidance, these urban areas flourished, becoming crucial nodes in the network of her expanding kingdom.

In addition to economic reforms, Teuta placed considerable emphasis on strengthening the military capabilities of Illyria. She focused on enhancing the army, ensuring it was well-equipped and trained to meet the challenges of the time. But perhaps her most innovative military venture was the creation of a formidable naval fleet. Teuta commissioned the construction of Liburnian ships, a design known for its speed and agility, which became the backbone of her naval power.

Through strategic conquests and diplomatic maneuvering, Teuta significantly expanded the borders of her kingdom. Her most notable military success came with the defeat of the Greek army and the subsequent capture of Phoenicia, the wealthiest and most influential city in the Epirus region. This victory not only solidified her control over the Adriatic Sea but also extended her influence to the Ionian Sea. Her dominance over these crucial maritime routes led her people to bestow upon her the title "Queen of Seas," a testament to her unparalleled naval prowess.

However, it was not just her conventional naval forces that garnered attention. Teuta's most infamous and feared asset was the fleet of Illyrian pirates. Piracy, intriguingly, was not only legal in Illyria but also considered a respectable and viable profession. Teuta granted these pirates unrestrained freedom to operate across the Mediterranean Sea, which they did with ruthless efficiency. Their activities not only contributed to the wealth of Illyria but also served as a strategic tool in asserting Teuta's dominance over the seas.

This rapid political and military empowerment of Teuta and her kingdom did not go unnoticed. The Roman Senate, in particular, viewed her ascension and the expansion of her influence with growing concern. Rome, a burgeoning power in the region, found the rivalry posed by such a formidable and ambitious woman ruler unacceptable. Teuta's successes, her control of key maritime routes, and her sanctioning of piracy presented a direct challenge to Roman interests and hegemony in the Mediterranean. As a result, tensions began to escalate between Illyria and Rome, setting the stage for a dramatic and historically significant confrontation.

The Roman Republic, emboldened by its recent and historic victory at Carta-gena, began to shift its imperial gaze towards the east, eyeing its neighbors for expansion. Among these, Illyria, with its significant maritime holdings and strategic coastal positions, emerged as a key target for Rome. The importance of Illyria lay not just in its land but more crucially in its control over vital sea routes. Roman senators, seeking to justify their expansionist agenda, seized upon the frequent attacks on Roman merchant ships by Illyrian pirates as a casus belli for their next military campaign.

Initially, Rome opted for a diplomatic approach to resolve the issue. The Senate dispatched two ambassadors to Illyria with the mission of negotiating with Queen Teuta and persuading her to curb the pirate activities. However, upon their arrival, they were met with a staunch refusal from the queen. Teuta informed the Roman envoys that piracy, far from being a criminal activity, was a legally sanctioned and integral part of the Ardiaean Kingdom's maritime strategy.

The situation escalated dramatically when Teuta, in a bold and unprecedented move, seized the Roman emissaries' ships. In an even more shocking turn of events, she detained one of the ambassadors and executed the other. This blatant act of defiance and hostility provided Rome with the perfect pretext to declare war on Illyria.

Queen Teuta, renowned for her military acumen and bravery, prepared for the inevitable conflict. She fortified the entire Illyrian coastline, setting up robust defenses against the anticipated Roman invasion. Despite being outnumbered — the Roman army was reportedly twice the size of the Illyrian forces — Teuta and her army managed to win several battles, showcasing their formidable fighting spirit and tactical prowess.

However, the Romans, known for their strategic cunning, resorted to various subterfuges to gain an upper hand in the conflict. The most significant of these was the betrayal of Teuta by one of her most trusted and powerful commanders, Demetrius of Pharos. Demetrius, harboring ambitions for the throne himself, switched allegiances, significantly undermining Teuta's position.

Despite this treachery and facing increasingly insurmountable odds, Teuta and her forces continued to valiantly resist the Roman onslaught for an additional six months. The relentless Roman campaign, however, gradually wore down Illyrian resistance. Eventually, Teuta, recognizing the futility of further resistance and seeking to avoid the potential fall of Scutari (modern-day Shkodra), the capital of the Ardiaean kingdom, to the Romans, was compelled to negotiate a peace treaty.

The terms of the peace forced Queen Teuta into a significant retreat. She withdrew to the Illyrian city of Rizan, relinquishing much of her kingdom's territory and influence to the Romans. This marked a turning point in the history of Illyria, as Roman domination began to take hold in the region.

Despite her defeat, Queen Teuta of Illyria displayed remarkable resilience and diplomatic skill in her negotiations with the Roman envoys. Understanding the critical situation her kingdom was in, she astutely managed to secure more favorable terms in the peace treaty with Rome. This negotiation was pivotal for Illyria, as it provided a crucial breathing space for the kingdom to recover both economically and militarily. This period of recuperation and rebuilding laid the groundwork for a resurgence of Illyrian strength, eventually leading to a renewed resistance against Roman dominance in what would be known as the Second Illyrian War. However, the historical records regarding Teuta's role in this later conflict are sparse and unclear.

What is even more enigmatic is the fate of Queen Teuta after these pivotal negotiations. The most widely circulated account, steeped more in legend than in verifiable fact, suggests a dramatic and tragic end for the queen. According to popular lore, Teuta, overwhelmed by the loss of her kingdom and her reduced circumstances, chose to end her life by leaping off a cliff into the Bay of Kotor, located in modern-day Risan, Montenegro.

This legendary act of despair is said to have left a lasting curse on Risan. The town, unlike its neighbors, is believed to have been deprived of a maritime heritage as a direct consequence of Teuta's tragic demise. However, the true circumstances of her death remain shrouded in mystery, with no historical evidence to confirm or refute the tales of her dramatic final act.

Queen Teuta's impact on history, despite her tragic end, was profound and enduring. Her legacy lived on in the spirit of Illyrian resistance against Rome. Even after her departure from the political scene, Illyria continued to challenge Roman authority. It was not until the Third Illyrian War in 168 B.C. that Rome finally managed to decisively subdue the region. Teuta's reign, her remarkable rise, her valiant resistance against one of the ancient world's greatest powers, and her eventual fall, left an indelible imprint on the annals of history, symbolizing the resilience and fighting spirit of Illyria.

Demetrius of Pharos

Demetrius of Pharos stands as a compelling yet enigmatic figure in the tapestry of ancient Mediterranean history. Existing in the shadows of the late 3rd century B.C.E., his life story unfolds like a classic tale of political intrigue and personal ambition. The obscurity surrounding his birth—whether he hailed from Greek or Illyrian lineage, or perhaps a fusion of both—only adds to the mystique of his character. Born or raised on the island of Pharos, now known as Hvar in modern-day Croatia, he grew up in a Hellenic colony, suggesting a strong Greek influence in his early life. Yet, the lack of concrete details about his early years leaves much to historical speculation.

Demetrius's linguistic abilities, fluently speaking both ancient Greek and Illyrian, indicate a man deeply entrenched in the cultural confluence of his time. This linguistic dexterity would have been an invaluable asset in the multicultural landscape of the ancient Mediterranean. It suggests a man who was as much at ease in the corridors of Greek power as in the rugged territories of the Illyrian tribes.

His ascent to power is largely tied to the tumultuous events surrounding the Illyrian Wars. Before the First Illyrian War (229-228 B.C.E.), Demetrius had already established himself as a ruler of Pharos, wielding considerable influence in the region. His governance of Pharos under the aegis of King Agron of Illyria as a governor or vassal lord signifies his prominent standing within Illyrian society, possibly as a dynast or a high-ranking noble.

Demetrius's role in the capture and control of Corcyra (Corfu) in 229 B.C.E. was a defining moment in his career. Entrusted with the leadership of an Illyrian garrison on the island, he quickly grasped Corcyra's strategic significance. The island, a critical node in the network of maritime routes connecting the Italian and Balkan Peninsulas and the Adriatic and Ionian Seas, was a coveted prize in the Mediterranean. Recognizing its value, Demetrius seized the opportunity to expand his power base, using his position to distance himself from the Illyrian queen Teuta.

In a bold and cunning move, Demetrius initiated secret negotiations with the Romans. He promised to hand over Corcyra without a fight, in exchange for Roman support in his bid to rule over the Illyrian coastal regions. This strategic alignment with Rome was a testament to his shrewd understanding of the larger geopolitical chessboard. His ability to pivot and align with the rising power of Rome speaks volumes about his political acumen and ambition.

The Hellenic citizens of Corcyra, sensing a shift in the political winds, threw their support behind Demetrius's overtures to the Roman Republic. Their preference for the Republic's more favorable stance on Hellenic commerce, as opposed to the authoritarian rule of the Illyrian Queen Teuta, was a significant factor in this alliance. Demetrius, astutely recognizing this sentiment, facilitated communication between the Corcyran Greeks and Rome, sending delegations to express their collective interests.

This convergence of interests set the stage for the Romans' decisive intervention in 229 B.C.E., marking the commencement of the First Illyrian War. A formidable Roman fleet, consisting of 200 ships under the command of Consul Gn. Fulvius Centumalus, made its way to Corcyra. Upon arrival, they found the island ready to fulfill Demetrius's promise of surrender. The Illyrian garrison stationed on the island, under pressure from both Demetrius and the Hellenic citizens, capitulated to the Roman forces. This pivotal moment not only marked the downfall of Queen Teuta's influence in the region but also highlighted the strategic cunning of Demetrius, who deftly maneuvered to align himself with the emerging Roman power.

In a dramatic turn of events, Demetrius joined the Roman ranks, where he was received as a valuable asset, given his extensive knowledge of the Illyrian monarchy. His decision to side with Rome was a calculated move, paving the way for his future ambitions. He accompanied the Roman forces as they marched towards the vital city of Apollonia (modern-day Pojan near Fier), another Hellenic colony. This city, too, welcomed the Romans, eagerly accepting their protection and forming an alliance. The involvement of the other Roman consul, Lucius Postumus Albinus, commanding a force of 20,000 infantry and 200 cavalry, only added to the gravity of the Roman campaign.

The Roman military successes rapidly shifted the balance of power in the region. By the spring of 228 B.C.E., the embattled Illyrian Queen was compelled to sign a peace treaty, severely limiting her realm's territorial holdings and naval capabilities, and imposing a war indemnity. In the wake of these events, Demetrius, bolstered by Roman support, emerged as the ruler of the territories conquered by Rome during the war. This expanse, excluding Corcyra and Apollonia, primarily consisted of the coastal regions along the Adriatic and northern Ionian Seas.

The aftermath of the First Illyrian War ushered in a period of political transition and uncertainty, particularly regarding the fate of Queen Teuta. Historical sources fall silent on her whereabouts or activities following the war, leading scholars to speculate about her eventual fate. This ambiguity has fueled theories that Demetrius of Pharos may have ascended to the Illyrian throne, taking over the reins of power sometime between 228-226 B.C.E. His rule, possibly extending beyond the coastal regions to the inland territories of the Ardiaei, signified a significant shift in the political landscape of the region.

Demetrius's rule was primarily concentrated in the area stretching from Scodra (modern-day Shkodër) to Lissus (present-day Lezhë). In a strategic move to consolidate his power and legitimize his rule, Demetrius married

Triteuta, the widow of King Agron and the mother of the young Illyrian heir, Pinnes. This marriage was more than a personal union; it was a calculated political maneuver to strengthen his claim over the Illyrian kingdom of the Ardiaei. Despite this, Demetrius's rule was not universally accepted or unchallenged. He seemed to be in a constant struggle for legitimacy and control, sharing power with Scerdilaidas, a former commander under Queen Teuta and possibly another Illyrian dynast. This duality in governance underscored the inherent challenges of ruling the Illyrians, a diverse and often fractious amalgamation of tribes with a history of intense internal rivalry.

In terms of foreign policy, Demetrius initially adopted a cautious approach towards Rome and other Hellenic states, keenly aware of the delicate balance of power. However, as time progressed, he began to perceive a diminishing interest from Rome in the Illyrian region. This perceived indifference, coupled with the Roman preoccupation with the Gallic/Celtic invasion of Italy in 225 B.C.E., which Polybius interpreted as a sign of Roman vulnerability, prompted a shift in Demetrius's stance. He began to reassess his alliance with Rome, concluding that the friendship with the Roman Republic was insufficient to fulfill his personal ambitions and expansionist objectives in the region.

This reassessment marked a turning point in Demetrius's relationship with Rome. Feeling emboldened by the apparent Roman distraction and crisis, he started pursuing his own political and military agenda more aggressively, acting independently of Roman interests. His focus shifted towards forging alliances with other foreign powers, moving away from his previous role as a Roman ally. This strategic pivot in Demetrius's foreign policy reflects a nuanced understanding of the changing geopolitical realities of the time and highlights his ambition to establish himself as a dominant force in the region.

During the period when Rome was preoccupied with the Gallic/Celtic conflict (225-222 B.C.E.), Demetrius of Pharos seized the opportunity to expand his influence and control in the Illyrian region. His expansionist ambitions led him to the areas of Atintania, presumably situated east of Apollonia, and Dassaretis, located further southeast. In a strategic move, Demetrius persuaded the Atintani, an Illyrian tribe, to break away from Roman allegiance and come under his protection. Additionally, Dassaretis, a key region for facilitating Illyrian-Macedonian communication, gradually succumbed to Demetrius's control.

During this period of expansion, Demetrius's activities were not limited to territorial conquests. As recorded by the ancient historian Appian, he collaborated with the Istri, natives of the Istrian peninsula, in conducting naval raids along the Adriatic Sea. These raids targeted Roman grain ships, which were crucial for supplying the Roman army engaged in battles in Cisalpine Gaul. This aggressive maneuvering against Rome's interests indicates a bold and defiant stance by Demetrius.

Between 225 and 223 B.C.E., Demetrius forged an alliance with the Macedonian regent Antigonus III Doson, who ruled from 229 to 221 B.C.E. This alliance was likely aimed at extending Demetrius's influence southward into mainland Hellas. The collaboration with the Macedonian king facilitated Demetrius's advance and control over the strategic region of Dassaretis, located in present-day southeastern Albania. Antigonus III Doson, harboring his own expansionist ambitions, sought to reassert Macedonian dominance over Hellas and strengthen the Macedonian state. In 223 B.C.E., Demetrius contributed a contingent of 1,600 Illyrian soldiers to Antigonus's mixed force in a campaign against Spartan King Cleomenes III in the Peloponnese. A year later, in the pivotal Battle of Sellasia in Laconia, Demetrius and his forces played a crucial role in the Macedonian victory over the Spartans, leading to the Macedonian occupation of Sparta. In return for his support, Demetrius secured control over Dassaretis and possibly gained influence over other territories in southern Illyria and the neighboring region of Paeonia.

In 221 B.C.E., the Roman Republic launched a brief campaign against the Istri, who were accused of raiding Roman grain ships in collaboration with Demetrius. However, Demetrius himself remained untouched by this campaign, casting doubt on the extent of his involvement with the Istrians, as suggested by Appian. Meanwhile, the Macedonian King Antigonus, fresh from his victory over Sparta, met his end in battle against the Illyrians under Scerdilaidas in northwestern Macedonia. This conflict underscored the deep divisions between the Illyrian factions led by Scerdilaidas and Demetrius.

Following the death of Antigonus, Demetrius sought to maintain a cordial relationship with his successor, Philip V. The young Macedonian ruler, inheriting his father's favorable view of Demetrius, was unable to provide military support for Demetrius in his impending conflict with Rome. This development left Demetrius in a precarious position, having lost a powerful ally and facing the looming prospect of war against a resurgent Roman Republic.

In the early months of 220 B.C.E., the Illyrian maritime campaign, spearheaded by Demetrius of Pharos and Scerdilaidas, commenced with a fleet of 90 lembi (swift naval vessels) setting sail southward from Lissus. This maneuver, as chronicled by the historian Polybius, was a direct violation of the Roman-Illyrian settlement established in 228 B.C.E., which expressly restricted Illyrian naval activity south of Lissus. The initial target of this Illyrian incursion was Pylos, a town located in the southwestern Peloponnese, also known as Navarino. The Illyrians laid siege to Pylos, launching a vigorous assault, but ultimately failed to capture the city. Following their unsuccessful siege, the Illyrian fleet split into two factions. Scerdilaidas chose to retreat northward, while Demetrius, with 50 ships, persisted in his campaign, navigating around the Peloponnesus to the Cyclades.

In the Cyclades, Demetrius's fleet embarked on a series of lucrative raids, pillaging multiple islands. These raids not only bolstered Demetrius's resources but also expanded his influence in the region. After these successful yet controversial exploits, Demetrius sailed to Cenchreae (modern-day Kechries) in the Saronic Gulf. It was here that Taurion, a commander of the Achaean League, approached Demetrius with a proposition. Polybius recounts this encounter, noting Taurion's plea for Demetrius to aid the Achaeans by transporting his fleet across the Isthmus of Corinth to launch a surprise attack on the Aetolians. Demetrius, having profited from his expeditions but also seeking to avoid confrontation with the pursuing Rhodian fleet, was receptive to Taurion's proposal, especially given Taurion's commitment to finance the transportation of the boats.

The strategic move to traverse the Isthmus was both innovative and tactically astute. The use of the diolkos, an ancient trackway designed to transport boats overland, allowed Demetrius's fleet to bypass the lengthy and perilous journey around the Peloponnese, providing a quicker and safer route back to the Ionian Sea. This method not only shortened their return voyage but also offered a tactical escape from potential retaliation by the Rhodians, who were mobilizing against Demetrius due to his raids in the Cyclades.

However, despite successfully transporting his fleet across the Isthmus, Demetrius's plan to ambush the Aetolians was thwarted by timing; he missed their crossing by a mere two days. Consequently, Demetrius redirected his efforts, conducting raids along the Aetolian coast before returning to Corinth. This episode in Demetrius's career exemplifies his adaptability and resourcefulness, characteristics that defined his approach to naval warfare and political maneuvering. His willingness to engage in bold and unconventional strategies not only highlights his military acumen but also underscores the dynamic and often unpredictable nature of naval warfare in the ancient Mediterranean.

In 220 B.C.E., classical sources detail further actions by Demetrius of Pharos that were in direct opposition to the interests of the Roman Republic, this time focusing on his land-based military endeavors. Demetrius, already in control of the Illyrian region of Atintania, advanced into Dassaretis, from where he launched an assault on the lands of the Parthini, an Illyrian tribe under Roman protection, and the nearby territory of Apollonia. These aggressive actions of Demetrius were later used as key components in the Roman casus belli against him.

The Roman Republic, viewing these incursions as a significant breach of their interests in the region, summoned Demetrius to appear before the Senate to answer for his actions. However, Demetrius, likely aware that his appearance would not alter the Romans' stance against him, chose not to comply. Consequently, the Roman Senate resolved to initiate another military campaign in Illyria, marking the onset of the Second Illyrian War in 219 B.C.E. For this campaign, Rome assigned its two consuls of the year, Lucius Aemilius Paullus and Marcus Livius Salinator, indicating the high priority and seriousness with which they approached the conflict. The Roman military force dispatched was likely comparable in size and strength to that utilized in the First Illyrian War.

Demetrius, anticipating Roman retaliation, had evidently learned from his experiences in the First Illyrian War. He is believed to have established an efficient intelligence network along the coast, which enabled him to be well-informed about the Roman movements. Upon learning of the Roman approach, Demetrius initiated a defensive strategy focused on two key locations: Dimale/Dimallum (present-day Krotinë) and Pharos. These cities were likely the southern and northern limits of his domain. Polybius records that Demetrius fortified Dimale/Dimallum with a significant garrison and necessary supplies. In other cities, he eliminated those who opposed him, installing loyalists in positions of power. Meanwhile, he himself, along with six thousand of his most elite troops, stationed themselves at Pharos.

The Roman forces, upon their arrival in Illyria, targeted Dimale with their full might, recognizing that capturing this stronghold would demoralize the Illyrian forces loyal to Demetrius. This strategy proved effective, and Dimale fell to the Romans within a week. Following this victory, local tribes and leaders quickly pledged their allegiance to the Romans, establishing treaties and agreements. The Roman campaign then proceeded northwards towards Pharos, where Demetrius had taken refuge. Through a well-executed stratagem, the Romans successfully captured Pharos. However, Demetrius, realizing the futility of his situation, managed to escape aboard a ship waiting in a concealed location and fled to Actium. There, he sought refuge with Philip V of Macedon, who had inherited the friendly relations previously established between Demetrius and Antigonus and had also engaged with Scerdilaidas during the winter of 220-219 B.C.E.

As a result of these events, Demetrius found himself a fugitive in Macedonian territory under the protection of Philip V. Meanwhile, the Roman forces, having taken Pharos, demolished the city and proceeded to assert control over the remaining parts of the Illyrian coast. They established or renewed agreements with the principal native tribes and cities, effectively expanding their influence in the region. This sequence of events highlights the volatile nature of ancient Mediterranean politics, where allegiances shifted rapidly, and military prowess often determined the fate of entire regions.

In the year 217 B.C.E., the Roman Republic, continuing its efforts to curb the influence of Demetrius of Pharos, sent envoys to Macedonia with a demand that would test the sovereignty and diplomatic resolve of the Macedonian kingdom. The Romans audaciously demanded the extradition of Demetrius, a request that King Philip V of Macedon, valuing his kingdom's autonomy and the strategic counsel of Demetrius, flatly refused. By this time, Demetrius had ingratiated himself deeply within the Macedonian court, becoming a trusted advisor to Philip, especially valued for his insights into Roman strategies and politics.

In June of that same year, while attending the Nemean festival in Argos, King Philip received startling news of Rome's defeat at the Battle of Lake Trasimene, a significant victory for Hannibal of Carthage in the Second Punic War. Initially, Philip shared this information only with Demetrius, recognizing him as his most reliable confidant. Seizing the moment, Demetrius advised the Macedonian king to quickly broker peace with the Aetolians and redirect his military efforts towards Illyria. He envisioned that by gaining control of the Illyrian coast and its strategic ports, Macedonia could effectively collaborate with Carthaginian forces against Rome. Demetrius's counsel to Philip, as recorded by Polybius, underscored the ambitious vision he had for Macedonia's role in the broader geopolitical landscape:

"For Greece is already entirely obedient to you, and will remain so: the Achaeans from genuine affection; the Aetolians from the terror which their disasters in the present war have inspired them. Italy, and your crossing into it, is the first step in the acquisition of universal empire, to which no one has a better claim than yourself. And now is the moment to act when the Romans have suffered a reverse."

Polybius reflects on Demetrius's motives, suggesting that his counsel was not primarily out of loyalty to Philip, but rather driven by his own antagonism towards Rome and a personal ambition to reclaim his rule over Pharos. Philip, convinced by Demetrius's arguments, embarked on a campaign to seize control of the Illyrian coast. In 215 B.C.E., an alliance was formed between Macedonia and Carthage against Rome. Notably, the treaty included a clause mentioning Demetrius, stipulating that Roman control over key Illyrian territories, including Corcyra, Apollonia, Epidamnus, Pharos, Dimale, Parthini, and Atintania, should cease, and that Demetrius's allies in Roman territory should be returned to him. However, this envisioned scenario never materialized, and Demetrius was not reinstated as ruler in Illyria.

Polybius critiques Demetrius's character, highlighting his daring nature but poor judgment. This led to his downfall in 214 B.C.E. when, backed by Philip, his attempt to capture Messene failed disastrously, resulting in his death. His career, marked by audacious endeavors and a constant rivalry with Rome, exemplifies the complex dynamics of personal ambition, political maneuvers, and changing alliances in Hellenistic geopolitics.

Gentius

entius, the renowned king of the Illyrians, reigned from 181 to 167
B.C.E. and emerged from the royal lineage of the Ardiaei tribe, being
the son of Pleuratus and Eurydice. His realm, often referred to as the
Kingdom of Illyria or the Kingdom of the Ardiaei, thrived during a tumultuous
period marked by the expanding influence of the Roman Republic over the
Illyrian coast and Macedon. Renowned for his leadership during the Third
Illyrian War, Gentius fiercely resisted Roman encroachment between 168 and
167 B.C.E., an episode that stands out in the annals of history.

Gentius, a figure with significant but still limited classical documentation
compared to other contemporaries in the Roman and Hellenic world, had a
complex family dynamic. His brother Plator and half-brother Caravantius,
from his mother Eurydice, played roles in his narrative. Succeeding his father
Pleuratus III, who ruled from 200 to 181 B.C.E. and maintained a loyal, vassal-
like relationship with Rome, Gentius charted a markedly different course. He
aspired for regional supremacy and strove for near-complete autonomy from
Roman control, working towards centralizing monetary, fiscal, and military
systems across Illyrian territories.

Historical accounts, such as those by Polybius, often painted Gentius in a harsh
light, suggesting he ruled with cruelty and engaged in licentious acts, fueled
by a lifestyle of constant intoxication. This portrayal includes the accusation
of fratricide against his brother Plator, followed by Gentius's marriage to
Plator's betrothed, Etleva/Etuta, the daughter of Monunius, the Dardanian

king. While some of these accounts could be exaggerated, reflective of Roman biases against the Illyrians, the marriage is corroborated by other classical sources. This alliance, formed a year before the outbreak of the war against Rome, was likely a strategic move by Gentius to consolidate regional power.

Gentius initially positioned himself as an ally of Rome against Macedon, but gradually shifted towards a stance of neutrality or autonomy. This shift did not sit well with the Romans, who kept a vigilant eye on his actions, particularly after he allied with the Macedonian king Perseus.

The onset of hostilities between Rome and the Illyrian king Gentius, who had recently ascended to power over the Ardiaei, marked a significant turn in the historical narrative of the Adriatic region. In 180 B.C.E., the Roman praetor Lucius Duronis played a pivotal role in escalating tensions when he confiscated ten Illyrian ships owned by Gentius, bringing them to Brundisium (modern-day Brindisi). This act was followed by Duronis presenting a case before the Roman Senate, alleging that these Illyrian ships were engaged in piracy and involved in the abduction of Italian merchants in the eastern waters of the Adriatic Sea. Gentius himself was directly accused of orchestrating these illicit activities. Moreover, the Romans held Gentius accountable for the capture of Roman and Italian ships and the imprisonment of their crews on the island of Corcyra Negra (present-day Korčula).

However, the piracy accusations against the Illyrians were largely seen as a contrivance, a narrative perpetuated by Roman propaganda. The depiction of Illyrians as perennial perpetrators of piratical raids in the Adriatic and Ionian Seas had been a recurring theme, predating the various Illyrian-Roman conflicts. This aggressive diplomatic stance by the Republic towards Gentius suggested a broader strategy, possibly indicating Roman preparations for another military campaign against the Illyrians, as well as other independent and semi-independent entities across the Balkans. This expansionist agenda of Rome towards the eastern Adriatic was set to culminate with their eventual triumph over both Gentius's Illyrian kingdom and the kingdom of Macedon by 167 B.C.E.

Contrary to the Roman claims, it is highly improbable that Gentius was actively engaging in piracy against Roman vessels. Seeking complete independence from Rome did not necessarily equate to initiating maritime conflicts. As a new ruler, Gentius would have been more inclined towards consolidating his position rather than provoking a formidable power like Rome. Acknowledging the criticality of these accusations, Gentius dispatched an Illyrian delegation to the Roman Senate. Their mission was to refute the allegations of piracy and the abduction of Roman ships and merchants. This diplomatic endeavor appears to have been effective, as there are no records of subsequent punitive actions or penalties levied against Gentius. Consequently, the Illyrian ruler was able to focus on reinforcing his domestic authority.

Upon ascending to the Illyrian throne, Gentius faced a significant geopolitical shift with the Dalmatians, an Illyrian tribe occupying the Dalmatian coast. Previously under the control of Pleuratus III, they had established an independent state, separate from Gentius's rule. This secession, coupled with the threat of losing influence over other tribal lands, likely propelled Gentius to adopt a novel administrative approach, distinct from his predecessors.

The territorial extent of Gentius's kingdom was substantial and varied. In the northwest, it reached the lands of the Daorsi and encompassed the valley of the Naro (Neretva) river. The north and northeast bordered independent Illyrian entities, notably the Autariatae and the Dardanians. The eastern boundary traversed the Mount Scardos (Sharr mountains) and followed the lower course of the Drin River up to Lychnidos (Ohrid). The southern border, potentially representing a demarcation line between Illyrian and Roman territories, was more ambiguous. It likely originated in Lissus, ran along the upper course of the Ardaksan (Mati) river, reached the Candavie Mountains (Mountain of Polis), and eventually met the eastern border near Lake Lychnidos (Lake Ohrid).

Gentius restructured the internal territories of his kingdom into administrative units centered around key cities. These cities, along with their surrounding fortresses, were pivotal in safeguarding the regional centers and their administrative domains. Each main city and unit was overseen by a 'principa illyriorum,' an official appointed by the king. In the kingdom's central areas, a regional ruler may not have been necessary, as Gentius exercised direct authority.

Scodra (Shkodra) was selected by Gentius as his royal seat, elevating it to the capital of his kingdom and the hub of the Ardiaei. Before Gentius's reign, Scodra served as the center for the Labeatis tribe, who, following the establishment of the Illyrian royalty in Scodra, relocated their capital to Medeon (Medun). Besides Scodra and Medeon, Rhizon (Risan, near Kotor) was another significant administrative unit. Strategically located, Rhizon controlled the naturally protected Bay of Kotor, facilitating secure access to the eastern Adriatic. Small fortresses dotting the bay's perimeter bolstered its security and control.

Southeast of Scodra lay the lands of the Penestae, presumably another administrative unit. Their capital, Uscana, has an elusive historical footprint, with its precise location yet to be definitively established. Classical sources suggest its vicinity to modern Kicevo. Uscana, encircled by several fortresses, held geostrategic significance as the southeasternmost part of the Illyrian kingdom. Its location, situated between the Illyrians of Gentius and the Macedonians, provided a crucial communication corridor.

King Gentius's administrative reform, while extensive, did not extend comprehensively into the more mountainous and remote areas of his kingdom. These regions, characterized by their rugged terrain and lack of urban development, were not conducive to the establishment of centralized administrative structures. Instead, small fortresses, often the seats of local tribal chieftains, were the primary form of governance in these highland areas. The sparse population and challenging geography made the implementation of a structured administrative system both impractical and unnecessary.

Nicholas Hammond, a noted historian drawing upon classical sources including Livy, provides a detailed analysis of the internal composition of Gentius's kingdom, shedding light on its diverse tribal makeup. According to Hammond, the kingdom comprised various tribes, each with its unique geographical and cultural identity. These included the Pirustae Dassaretiorum, the Rhizonitae, and the Olciniatae, who notably rebelled while Gentius was still secure in power. The Daorsi, situated near the river Naro opposite Pharos, shifted allegiance to the Roman side. Other tribes such as the Scodrenses, the Dassarenses, and the Selepitani, along with the broadly categorized "ceteri Illyrii," were tributaries to Gentius.

Hammond further elaborates on the locations and identities of these tribes. The Pirustae, possibly the same as Strabo's Peirustae, were located north of the Ardiaei. The Rhizonitae occupied the area around the Gulf of Rhizon (now Kotor). The Olciniatae, whose name is preserved in the modern city of Ulcinj, were southwest of Scodra. The Scodrenses, distinct from the Labeates as noted by Pomponius Mela, were based around Scodra. The Selepitani, however, remain somewhat enigmatic due to the lack of detailed historical records.

This diverse and scattered array of tribes under Gentius's dominion provides a glimpse into the nature of the Ardiaean kingdom during its decline. Hammond's summary paints a picture of a kingdom composed of various tribes, each with its own distinct geographic and cultural characteristics, loosely united under the rule of King Gentius.

This ambitious initiative began with the overhaul of the Scodra minting operations. He ceased the production of the existing coinage and introduced new royal coins. These coins featured the king's portrait on one side and the emblematic Illyrian ship on the other, replacing the city's legend with the king's title and name. Additionally, the existing coin that bore a helmet and shield, a design dating back to the era of Pleuratus III, was also redesigned. While retaining its original symbols, this coin was updated to include Gentius's title and name, reinforcing his authority and presence throughout his realm.

The monetary reforms were not limited to Scodra. Gentius extended these changes to the minting factory in Lissus, effectively ending the city's monetary independence and integrating it into the royal monetary system. This move created a cohesive monetary system within the central coastal regions of the kingdom, particularly in areas where Scodra and Lissus served as pivotal minting centers. The unified currency consisted of three primary coins: the coin depicting the king and the Illyrian ship, the redesigned coin with the helmet and shield, and a smaller denomination previously minted in Lissus, now bearing the king's insignia. The first two types, especially the one with the king's portrait and ship, held the highest value and were produced in Scodra, underscoring their significance.

However, this monetary unification was not all-encompassing. The peripheral areas of Gentius's kingdom, such as Rhizon (Kotor) and Lychnidos (Ohrid), maintained a degree of monetary autonomy. Rhizon continued minting its own silver coins, while Lychnidos persisted in producing its bronze coins adorned with a shield and a segment of a ship. This autonomy granted to these cities, despite being within the administrative reach of Gentius's kingdom, indicates that the king's authority might not have been as influential in these outlying regions. Furthermore, the northern tribes like the Labeates and Daorsi retained their independent coinage.

The geographic production of Gentius's royal coins may have been confined, but their circulation extended far beyond, permeating even the most remote and mountainous regions of his kingdom. This widespread distribution is evidenced by the discovery of these coins in various locations, including northern Montenegro and the vicinities of ancient Dyrrachium and Apollonia. Such findings indicate not only a high level of trade activity but also the successful integration of distant areas into the kingdom's monetary and economic system. The introduction of a standardized currency significantly facilitated trade, contributing to an increase in the volume of commercial exchanges throughout the kingdom.

The financial implications of these monetary reforms under King Gentius were substantial, as suggested by historical accounts, particularly those of Titus Livius (Livy). Livy notes that the Romans, upon their victory over the Illyrians, seized a significant royal treasure from Gentius, comprising 19 pounds of silver, 27 pounds of gold, 13,000 denarii, and 120,000 Illyrian drachmas. This considerable accumulation of wealth by Gentius likely stemmed from various sources, including fees levied on large royal landowners and substantial taxes imposed on his subjects. A major factor driving this concentration of wealth was the need to counter the looming Roman threat. The Roman Senate, as early as 178 B.C.E. – merely two years after Gentius's accession – had dispatched a fleet of 10 ships to patrol the Adriatic waters from Ancona to Tarentum, signaling their strategic interest in the region.

To confront this challenge, Gentius was compelled to allocate substantial resources for maintaining a formidable military presence. The royal coins played a crucial role in this endeavor, being distributed widely among the military forces and the workers in the shipyards. This circulation of coins into the economy was particularly pronounced during the mobilization for war against Rome. At the onset of the conflict, Gentius's regular army was approximately 15,000 strong, with a significant concentration of troops around Lissus. Moreover, the eventual capture of 220 Illyrian ships by the Romans at the war's conclusion underscores the substantial efforts and resources invested by Gentius in bolstering his naval capabilities.

In 172 B.C.E., the attention of the Roman Republic was once again drawn to Gentius, the King of Illyria. This renewed focus was prompted by a delegation from the island of Issa, a Hellenic colony, which presented itself before the Roman Senate. The Issaeans leveled serious accusations against Gentius, claiming he had attacked their lands on two separate occasions. Additionally, they alleged a conspiracy between Gentius and the Macedonian King Perseus against Rome. However, these claims appear questionable, as there is no substantial evidence to support the Issaeans' assertion of an alliance between Gentius and Perseus at this juncture. An Illyrian delegation was sent to counter these accusations, but the Romans dismissed their arguments with disdain. It seemed as though the Romans had already made up their minds to intervene in the Adriatic region, targeting not only the Illyrians but also the Macedonians.

By 170 B.C.E., the domains of Macedonian King Perseus began to encroach upon those of Gentius, particularly after Perseus's successful military campaign against the Romans in the region of the Penestae. This campaign temporarily alleviated the Roman threat from the west and opened a direct line of communication with King Gentius. Following his return to Stuberra (Prilep), Perseus initiated efforts to forge an alliance with Gentius against Rome. Polybius, the ancient historian, provides a detailed account of these diplomatic maneuvers:

Perseus sent envoys, including Pleuratus (not to be confused with Pleuratus III) and Adaeus of Beroea, to King Gentius. Their mission was to inform Gentius of Perseus's ongoing war against the Romans, Dardanians, Epirots, and Illyrians, and to propose an alliance with the Macedonians. The envoys traversed the challenging terrain of Mount Scardus and the so-called Desert Illyria, a region previously depopulated by the Macedonians to deter Dardanian invasions. Reaching Scodra, they learned that Gentius was in Lissus and sent a message to him. Gentius, showing initial interest in an alliance, cited a lack of resources and the impracticality of waging war against Rome without financial support as obstacles. The envoys returned to Perseus with Gentius's response.

Undeterred, Perseus sent the same envoys back to Gentius, seemingly ignoring Gentius's stated need for financial support. The envoys departed as Perseus and his army moved towards Hyscana. In a subsequent attempt, Perseus dispatched Hippias to Gentius to finalize an agreement, yet again neglecting the critical issue of financial support. Hippias returned with the report that Gentius was ready to engage in war against Rome if he received 300 talents and proper assurances.

Recognizing the strategic importance of Gentius's cooperation, Perseus sent Pantauchus, one of his closest advisors, with instructions to agree to the financial terms and exchange oaths of alliance. Pantauchus quickly persuaded Gentius to join forces with Perseus.

The negotiations between Perseus and Gentius spanned roughly a year. Classical sources suggest this prolonged period was partly due to Gentius's attempts to maximize financial and military gains. However, Gentius's hesitation might also be attributed to differing military strategies and objectives. While Perseus aimed for a decisive victory over Rome through military force, Gentius likely sought a more peaceful resolution that would allow him to maintain his kingship over the principal regions of his kingdom.

In 168 B.C.E., the Roman Republic initiated the Third Illyrian War by directing its military efforts against King Gentius. Roman generals Lucius Anicius and Appius Claudius were tasked with leading the campaign against the Illyrian ruler. In response, Gentius mobilized a force of approximately 15,000 soldiers, strategically positioning them around the city of Lissus. Concurrently, an Illyrian naval contingent engaged in raids along the coastlines of Dyrrachium and Apollonia. This offensive, however, was met with resistance when the Roman fleet, stationed at Apollonia, successfully repelled the Illyrian ships in a significant naval battle.

The critical and decisive confrontation of the war occurred near Scodra. Here, the Roman forces effectively overwhelmed the initial resistance put up by the Illyrians, leading to the eventual surrender of King Gentius and his remaining army. This rapid and decisive victory by the Romans was significant in bringing the Illyrian War to a swift conclusion.

Polybius, the ancient historian, provides a detailed account of the aftermath of the war:

Following the capture of Scodra, Lucius Anicius tasked Perperna with apprehending Gentius's close associates. Perperna promptly headed to Medeon, a city in Labeatia, and captured several key figures, including Etleva, Gentius's consort; his brother Caravantius; and his sons, Scerdiletus and Pleuratus. These captives were brought to the Roman camp at Scodra. Anicius, having effectively ended the Illyrian war in just thirty days, sent Perperna to Rome to announce this triumph. Shortly thereafter, King Gentius himself, along with his mother, queen, children, brother, and other notable Illyrians, were taken into Roman custody.

Gentius spent the remainder of his life in exile in Gubbio, located in the region of Perugia in Italy, until his death in 146 B.C.E. Apart from his military and political endeavors, Gentius is also remembered for his discovery of the medicinal properties of the plant Gentiana lutea, which was named after him. This plant, now a component in various beverages including the Aperol Spritz, was historically used as an antidote for venomous bites and for treating various wounds.

Gan Ning

Gan Ning, a historical figure of significant intrigue, hailed from Linjiang County, part of Ba Commandery, now known as Zhong County in modern-day Chongqing. However, the roots of his ancestry lay in Nanyang, Henan. His forebears had migrated from there to Ba Commandery, where they established their new home. In his youth, Gan Ning briefly embraced a conventional path, taking up a role as an accounting assistant in the local commandery office. This conventional stint was short-lived, as he soon resigned and returned home.

During his younger years, Gan Ning's vibrant energy and adventurous spirit led him to embody the role of a youxia, or vigilante. He became the charismatic leader of a band of rebellious young men, forging a life of roguery and plunder. This gang, armed with bows and crossbows, became notorious for their distinctive appearance: feathers adorning their hats and bells tied to their bodies, which jingled ominously, heralding their approach. This was not just a band of ordinary brigands; they had a flair for the dramatic. Gan Ning's infamy spread across Ba Commandery for his plundering escapades and ruthless actions.

Not only did Gan Ning lead his gang in raids on land, where they rode horses or traveled in chariots in a unique formation, but they also took to the waters. There, they sailed in light vessels that were linked together, displaying their mastery over both terrains. Their clothing was as flamboyant as their actions, designed to draw attention. At their stops, they would tie their boats with silk to the jetties, and upon departure, they would cut and abandon these silks, a testament to their lavish and extravagant lifestyle.

Gan Ning's interactions with local officials were complex. Some officials treated him with generosity, to which he responded with friendship and genuine affection. However, those who crossed him faced the wrath of his gang, often being robbed of their possessions. Even government officials were not immune to their marauding. Gan Ning continued this life of high-stakes banditry until he was over 20 years old.

His life took a significant turn after the death of Liu Yan, the governor of Yi Province, covering present-day Sichuan and Chongqing, in 194. Rebelling against Liu Yan's son and successor, Liu Zhang, Gan Ning found support from Liu He, an official from neighboring Jing Province, and Liu Zhang's subordinates, Shen Mi and Lou Fa. Despite their efforts, their rebellion was unsuccessful, forcing them to flee to Jing Province, marking yet another dramatic chapter in the life of this enigmatic figure.

He delved into the intellectual realm, immersing himself in the wisdom of the Hundred Schools of Thought, an era of great philosophical diversity in Chinese history. This intellectual journey marked a significant transformation in Gan Ning's life perspective and ambitions.

With a newfound sense of purpose, Gan Ning gathered a formidable force of 800 men and aligned himself with Liu Biao, the Governor of Jing Province, an area encompassing present-day Hubei and Hunan. They were stationed in Nanyang Commandery, where Liu Biao, a man of scholarly background, lacked expertise in military matters. During this period, China was engulfed in chaos, with numerous warlords vying for territorial control and empire hegemony in a relentless struggle for power.

As Gan Ning observed the unfolding turmoil, he realized that Liu Biao's leadership, hindered by his lack of military acumen, was destined for failure.

Fearing the implications this could have for his own future, Gan Ning contemplated a strategic move. He planned to head east with his followers towards the Wu region, then under the control of the warlords Sun Ce and later Sun Quan.

However, their journey was fraught with challenges. Upon reaching Jiangxia Commandery in eastern Jing Province, Gan Ning found the path to Wu territory blocked. Sun Quan was embroiled in a conflict with Liu Biao, rendering the border impassable. Left with no choice, Gan Ning and his men remained in Jiangxia, where they became subordinates of the commandery administrator, Huang Zu. Despite Gan Ning's capabilities, Huang Zu failed to recognize his talent, treating him with indifference for three long years.

The year 203 brought a pivotal moment. Sun Quan launched an attack on Huang Zu, culminating in the Battle of Xiakou. Displaying his exceptional skills as an archer, Gan Ning led a troop detachment to aid Huang Zu. In a critical moment, Gan Ning's arrow found its mark, killing Ling Cao, a colonel under Sun Quan, and saving Huang Zu's life. However, even this act of bravery did not alter Huang Zu's dismissive attitude towards Gan Ning.

Su Fei, an area commander under Huang Zu, saw Gan Ning's potential and repeatedly recommended him, but to no avail. Huang Zu's indifference went so far as to attempt to lure away Gan Ning's followers. This betrayal deeply unsettled Gan Ning.

Feeling trapped and undervalued, Gan Ning yearned for a change. Su Fei, understanding his frustration, devised a plan. He proposed to Huang Zu that Gan Ning be appointed chief of Zhu County, a challenging but potentially rewarding position. This appointment would be a stepping stone, allowing Gan Ning to carve out his own path. After securing Huang Zu's approval, Gan Ning gathered a loyal contingent of a few hundred men and set off for Zhu County. From there, they would eventually cross into the territories of Jiangdong, a journey that would open new chapters in Gan Ning's eventful life.

Upon arriving in Jiangdong with his followers, Gan Ning's fate took a significant turn. Recognizing his potential, Zhou Yu and Lü Meng introduced him to Sun Quan, their lord. Sun Quan, perceiving Gan Ning's exceptional abilities, welcomed him warmly, treating him as an old friend and recognizing his unique talents.

Gan Ning, seizing this opportunity, presented a well-thought-out strategic proposal to Sun Quan. He observed that the Han Empire was in decline, and the ambitious Cao Cao was poised to usurp the throne. Gan Ning pointed out the strategic importance of the southern territories of Jing Province, highlighting their accessibility and significance. He argued that Liu Biao, the current ruler of these lands, was on the brink of downfall and his sons lacked the capability to succeed him. Gan Ning urged Sun Quan to seize control of these territories before Cao Cao could.

His plan included an initial attack on Huang Zu, characterizing him as an inept and unpopular leader, burdened by aging, confusion, lack of resources, and disloyalty among his subordinates. Gan Ning highlighted Huang Zu's military weaknesses, such as damaged warships, neglected agriculture, and a disorderly army, making him an easy target. He proposed that, after defeating Huang Zu, Sun Quan could advance further west, secure Chu Pass, and expand his domain and influence, eventually preparing for an assault on Bashu.

Sun Quan was inclined to adopt Gan Ning's plan, but Zhang Zhao, one of his advisers, strongly opposed it, citing the instability of Wu's own territories. Undeterred, Gan Ning challenged Zhang Zhao's caution, comparing his responsibilities to those of the legendary Xiao He. He questioned Zhang Zhao's confidence in maintaining order, implying that such doubts were unbecoming of someone in his position.

Sun Quan, impressed by Gan Ning's boldness and strategic acumen, entrusted him with the planned campaign. In a symbolic gesture, Sun Quan raised his glass to Gan Ning, indicating his appointment as the leader of the upcoming military action against Huang Zu. He encouraged Gan Ning to develop a strategy to ensure victory and reassured him that his achievements would overshadow any criticisms from Zhang Zhao.

In the spring of 208, under Sun Quan's command, the forces advanced westward to Jiangxia Commandery, which is in the present-day Xinzhou District of Wuhan, Hubei. The campaign was a resounding success, resulting in the defeat and capture of Huang Zu and the acquisition of his troops. Gan Ning played a pivotal role in this victory and was subsequently appointed to command a garrison at Dangkou.

In the later years, between the late 200s and early 210s, Gan Ning found himself embroiled in a complex political situation. A revolt broke out against Liu Zhang, who had recently succeeded his father. Liu Zhang, facing this challenge, dispatched Zhao Wei, a key ally of his late father, to quell the uprising. Zhao Wei's efforts were successful, suppressing the rebels and forcing them to flee towards Jingzhou in the east, further illustrating the turbulent times in which Gan Ning navigated his military and political career.

Prior to the commencement of the military campaign against Huang Zu, Sun Quan had prepared with a measure of confidence, symbolized by two boxes designated for the heads of Huang Zu and Su Fei, a sign of his expectation of victory. Following the battle, Su Fei, who had been captured, sought to reach out to Gan Ning, aware of their past connection.

Gan Ning, upon hearing of Su Fei's predicament, expressed a momentary lapse of memory, indicating how the heat of battle had overshadowed his previous affiliations. However, the significance of his bond with Su Fei soon resurfaced. During a celebration of the victory, Gan Ning made a dramatic and heartfelt appeal to Sun Quan. He left his seat, knelt down, and kowtowed before Sun Quan until his forehead bled, tears streaming down his face. He implored Sun Quan to spare Su Fei's life, citing the deep debt of gratitude he owed him. Gan Ning emphasized that it was Su Fei who had played a crucial role in his survival and subsequent ability to serve Sun Quan.

Moved by Gan Ning's earnest plea, Sun Quan voiced concern about the possibility of Su Fei leaving once spared. To this, Gan Ning confidently assured that Su Fei would remain loyal and grateful for being spared from death, asserting that Su Fei would not seek his own doom. Gan Ning even offered his own life as a guarantee, stating he would replace Su Fei's head in the box should Su Fei betray their mercy. Convinced by Gan Ning's conviction, Sun Quan granted a pardon to Su Fei.

In the winter of 208–209, Gan Ning played a pivotal role in the Battle of Red Cliffs, serving under the command of Zhou Yu. They faced the formidable forces of Cao Cao and triumphed at Wulin. Following this victory, Gan Ning also participated in the subsequent Battle of Jiangling. In this encounter, Zhou Yu's forces attempted to overpower Cao Cao's general, Cao Ren, at Nan Commandery, near present-day Jiangling County, Hubei, but were initially unable to capture the city.

Gan Ning, demonstrating his strategic acumen, suggested leading a separate force to seize Yiling, near present-day Yichang, Hubei. He commenced this mission with only a few hundred soldiers, but his ranks swelled to around 1,000 after recruiting local men. Cao Ren, in response, sent a force of 5,000 to 6,000 troops to besiege Gan Ning at Yiling. The enemy constructed high towers and launched relentless arrow attacks on Yiling. Despite the fear this induced in his troops, Gan Ning remained composed.

Recognizing the need for reinforcements, Gan Ning sent a messenger to Zhou Yu, who, guided by Lü Meng's strategy, promptly led reinforcements to aid Gan Ning. Meanwhile, Ling Tong was tasked with defending their original position. This coordinated effort successfully lifted the siege at Yiling, with Zhou Yu, Lü Meng, and others playing critical roles in the operation. Ling

Tong, on his part, managed to effectively maintain his position during this critical period.

The protracted warfare ultimately took its toll on Cao Cao's resources and manpower, forcing him to order Cao Ren to abandon Nan Commandery. This strategic withdrawal allowed Sun Quan's forces to capture the commandery, marking another significant victory in their campaign. This series of events underscored Gan Ning's crucial role in Sun Quan's military endeavors, highlighting his strategic mind and fearless leadership in the face of daunting odds.

In the year 215, a significant disagreement arose between Sun Quan and his ally Liu Bei over the control of southern Jing Province, a dispute pivotal in the shifting allegiances and territorial claims of the era. The bone of contention lay in the division of three key commanderies: Changsha, Lingling (near present-day Yongzhou, Hunan), and Guiyang (near present-day Chenzhou, Hunan). Sun Quan, intent on asserting his dominion, dispatched Lü Meng and Ling Tong to seize these territories from Liu Bei. To fortify his position against any possible backlash, Sun Quan placed Lu Su in charge at Yiyang, a strategic location to counter Liu Bei's formidable general, Guan Yu, who oversaw his lord's interests in the southern parts of Jing Province.

Gan Ning, a key figure in Sun Quan's military cadre, joined Lu Su at Yiyang during this tense period. Guan Yu, boasting a significant force of 30,000 troops, had selected 5,000 of his elite soldiers and positioned them at shallow waters 10 li (approximately 5 kilometers) from Yiyang. He planned a night-time crossing of these shallows, a move that could potentially swing the strategic balance.

In response, Lu Su convened a council with his commanders to devise a strategy to counter Guan Yu. Despite having only 300 men under his command, Gan Ning boldly proposed to confront Guan Yu directly. He confidently assured Lu Su that with an additional 500 troops, he would deter Guan Yu from crossing the waters. If Guan Yu dared to advance, Gan Ning vowed to capture him.

Recognizing Gan Ning's bravery and tactical acumen, Lu Su granted him command of 1,000 troops. Under the cover of night, Gan Ning advanced towards Guan Yu's position. As anticipated by Gan Ning, Guan Yu refrained from crossing the shallows, choosing instead to establish camps in that area. The location thereafter came to be known as 'Guan Yu's Shallows', a testament to this standoff.

Sun Quan, impressed and pleased with Gan Ning's accomplishment in this tense military standoff, appointed him as the Administrator of Xiling Commandery, granting him oversight of the counties of Yangxin and Xiazhi, east of present-day Yangxin County, Hubei. This appointment was a significant recognition of Gan Ning's capabilities and contributions.

Earlier in 215, Gan Ning had demonstrated his valor in an assault on Cao Cao's garrison at Wan County, present-day Qianshan County, Anhui. He was assigned the critical task of scaling the fortress walls, a daring feat that he accomplished armed with a chain. Gan Ning's bold actions led to the capture of Wan County's defending commander, Zhu Guang. While Lü Meng was credited with the primary success of this operation, Gan Ning received high commendation for his role, leading to his promotion to the rank of General Who Breaks and Charges.

Later that same year, Gan Ning took part in Sun Quan's campaign aimed at seizing Hefei, a stronghold defended by Cao Cao's general, Zhang Liao. The siege of Hefei was challenging, marked by initial defeats and prolonged engagements. Sun Quan's inability to capture the city, compounded by the outbreak of a plague within his army, forced a strategic withdrawal. The retreat was staged in phases, with Sun Quan himself, accompanied by a small contingent including notable officers Lü Meng, Jiang Qin, Ling Tong, and Gan Ning, remaining at Xiaoyao Ford.

Zhang Liao, seizing this opportunity, launched a fierce counterattack, plunging Sun Quan's forces into disarray. Gan Ning, demonstrating his leadership and quick thinking, led a group of archers to counter the enemy's onslaught. Alongside Ling Tong and others, he fought valiantly to protect their lord. His command to beat war drums and blow horns was a crucial tactic to boost morale amidst the chaos. Although Sun Quan successfully escaped, his forces suffered significant losses.

In 217, two years after the previous conflict, the military landscape saw another dramatic escalation. Cao Cao, one of the most prominent warlords of the era, personally led a massive army, reportedly comprising 400,000 soldiers, to launch an assault on Sun Quan's stronghold at Ruxu. In response, Sun Quan mobilized a considerable force of about 70,000 troops to meet this formidable challenge. Among these troops, Gan Ning was entrusted with the command of the vanguard, a critical unit of 3,000 soldiers, underscoring his strategic importance in Sun Quan's military hierarchy.

Sun Quan, devising a covert strategy, gave Gan Ning a clandestine order to launch a night attack on the enemy. For this daring operation, Gan Ning handpicked 100 elite soldiers, men capable of executing such a high-risk mission. Prior to the battle, in a gesture of solidarity and encouragement, Sun Quan sent food and wine to Gan Ning and his men. After enjoying the feast, Gan Ning, in a display of boldness and camaraderie, poured wine into a silver bowl and drank heartily before offering it to one of his officers. The officer, initially hesitant to share the drink, was compelled by Gan Ning's assertive demeanor and his expression of equal respect for their lord and himself. This act of shared courage emboldened the troops, with each soldier partaking in the wine, symbolizing their unity and resolve.

As midnight neared, Gan Ning and his select group of 100 men executed the planned raid on Cao Cao's camp. They successfully destroyed defensive structures and eliminated dozens of enemy soldiers, creating chaos and confusion within Cao Cao's ranks. The enemy troops, taken aback by the sudden attack, lit up the camp with torches and sounded the alarm. However, by this time, Gan Ning and his men had skillfully retreated to their own camp, where they celebrated their successful raid with drumbeats, horn blasts, and triumphant shouts of "wansui!"

Later that night, Gan Ning visited an elated Sun Quan, who expressed his admiration for Gan Ning's bravery and the impact of his actions on Cao Cao. In recognition of his valor, Sun Quan rewarded Gan Ning with lavish gifts of 1,000 rolls of silk and 100 swords. He also drew a comparison between himself and Cao Cao, stating that just as Cao Cao had the formidable Zhang Liao, he had Gan Ning, a worthy match in military prowess. This successful defense led to Cao Cao's withdrawal from Ruxu after just over a month, a significant victory for Sun Quan. Following this, Gan Ning's reputation soared within Sun Quan's forces, leading to an increase of 2,000 troops under his command.

The details surrounding Gan Ning's death remain somewhat obscure in historical records. His biography in the Sanguozhi does not provide explicit details, only noting Sun Quan's deep lamentation at his passing. The Jiankang Shilu, another historical source, records that Gan Ning died in the winter of 215–216. However, the renowned Australian sinologist Rafe de Crespigny estimated Gan Ning's death to have occurred around the year 220. Regardless of the exact date, it is clear that Gan Ning's demise marked the end of a remarkable and storied military career, and his legacy continued to be honored and remembered by Sun Quan and the forces he had so valiantly served.

Eustace the Monk

Born circa 1170 AD as Eustace Busket, his life began in the rustic and picturesque surroundings near Boulogne, nestled in the northern reaches of France. This setting, a tapestry of feudal landscapes and burgeoning noble ambitions, was the cradle of Eustace's early years.

The saga of Eustace, as chronicled in the captivating "Romance of Eustace," a biographical romance penned by an anonymous poet from Picardy, France, between 1223 and 1284 AD, paints a picture of a man destined to transcend the ordinary. Eustace's birthplace, identified in the text as Corse, is believed to be Courset, a quaint hamlet situated a mere 19 kilometers (12 miles) from the bustling town of Boulogne.

Born into the family of Baudoin Busket, a figure of minor nobility in the County of Boulogne, Eustace's upbringing seemed unremarkable, akin to that of his peers among the minor nobility. Yet, beneath the surface of this seemingly mundane existence, the seeds of an extraordinary destiny were germinating.

Eustace's life took a dramatic and mystifying turn during his youth with a journey that would forever alter his path. Drawn to the ancient city of Toledo, Spain, a place renowned for its mystical and esoteric knowledge, Eustace embarked on a quest that was anything but ordinary. His purpose? To delve into the enigmatic and forbidden realms of black magic.

In the hushed whispers of legend, it is said that Eustace found his dark tutelage in the depths of a secluded cave, a place where the veil between the natural and supernatural was thin. Rumors, as dark and intriguing as the arts he studied, suggested that Eustace's mentor was none other than the Devil himself. Such was Eustace's prowess in these arcane studies that, by the end of his apprenticeship, he was unrivaled in France in the art of sorcery.

This extraordinary claim, however, stands alone, unsupported by other historical sources. It remains a tantalizing mystery whether the author of the "Romance of Eustace" crafted this narrative from the threads of imagination or drew upon some lost fragment of truth.

After his rumored foray into the shadowy world of black magic, Eustace embarked on a new chapter, one marked by spiritual devotion and monastic life. He joined the Benedictine order at Samer Abbey, situated a stone's throw away from Boulogne. The reasons behind this drastic shift in Eustace's life remain shrouded in mystery, though it's speculated that his status as a younger son in a noble family might have influenced this decision. While the tales of his study of dark arts might be taken with skepticism, what followed in his monastic life was equally, if not more, controversial.

Eustace's time at Samer Abbey was anything but typical for a monk. He quickly gained notoriety for his mischievous and rebellious behavior, often leading his fellow monks astray. His antics included encouraging monks to eat during periods of fasting, cursing during sacred recitations, and engaging in crude behavior such as flatulence in the cloisters. This peculiar fondness for flatulence, oddly enough, would resurface in later tales of his life. Despite his religious vows, Eustace proved to be a far cry from the ideal monk, earning the ironic epithet "Eustace the Monk."

His stay at the Abbey was brief and tumultuous. According to the "Romance of Eustace," he left the Benedictine order with a mission to seek justice for his father's murder from the Count of Boulogne. However, the chronicler Matthew Paris offers a different perspective, suggesting Eustace departed to secure an inheritance for his deceased brothers, though this claim is complicated by the fact that his brothers are said to have outlived him, surviving the Battle of Sandwich where Eustace met his demise.

Eustace's quest for justice led him to confront Hainfrois de Heresinghen, the alleged murderer of his father. In a dramatic turn of events, a duel was arranged, not between Eustace and Hainfrois, but rather between champions representing each. Eustace's champion was defeated, absolving Hainfrois in the eyes of the law. Disheartened and unable to avenge his father's death, Eustace then entered the service of Renaud de Dammartin, the Count of Boulogne.

As the count's seneschal, a role of significant responsibility and influence, Eustace managed various administrative and financial affairs. However, this position was not without its own set of trials and tribulations. Eustace's tenure was marred by accusations of financial misconduct, possibly instigated by Hainfrois, leading to a falling out with Count Renaud.

Following a tense confrontation with the legal system, Eustace, proclaiming his innocence, ultimately chose the path of a fugitive, fearing the harsh consequences of a perceived miscarriage of justice. Renaud, interpreting Eustace's flight as a tacit admission of guilt, branded him an outlaw, confiscated his property, and devastated his lands. In a dramatic turn of events, Eustace, fueled by a burning desire for retribution, transformed into a renegade, haunting the forests of Boulogne much like the legendary Robin Hood of English folklore.

Eustace's time as an outlaw was marked by a series of audacious and often humorous exploits. In one notorious incident, he cunningly deceived one of the count's knights. Masquerading as a woman, Eustace enticed the young knight with the promise of intimate favors in exchange for assistance onto his horse. The ruse culminated in Eustace releasing a loud fart as he was lifted, a distraction that allowed him to abscond with the knight's horse.

Another tale recounts how Eustace, in the guise of a leper, cunningly beguiled Count Renaud himself. Feigning infirmity, he persuaded Renaud to offer him alms, only to leap onto one of the count's horses and gallop away, leaving Renaud bewildered and outwitted.

However, not all of Eustace's adventures bore a light-hearted veneer. Some episodes took a decidedly darker tone. In one grim account, Eustace captured five of Renaud's men-at-arms, maiming four by severing their feet and releasing the fifth as a messenger bearing a chilling warning to the count. In another, Eustace ensnared a young boy, suspected to be a spy for the count, and mercilessly forced him to end his own life.

Despite the effectiveness of his guerrilla tactics in disrupting the count's affairs, Eustace recognized that his battle against Renaud had escalated to a dangerous new level with the latter's alliance with the French king. Now an adversary of both the count and the state, Eustace decided to flee to England, hoping to find refuge and purpose in the court of King John, particularly as France was then embroiled in conflict with England.

Eustace's allegiance to King John is believed to have commenced around 1205 AD. It was during this period that he transitioned from a land-bound outlaw to a fearsome pirate. Commanding the turbulent waters of the English Channel and the Strait of Dover, he targeted French vessels with relentless fervor. King John, recognizing Eustace's strategic prowess, entrusted him with the leadership of a formidable fleet of 30 ships, unleashing Eustace's maritime wrath upon the French.

The relationship between Eustace and King John of England was initially harmonious, with John granting Eustace considerable freedom on the high seas. Eustace leveraged this liberty to attack any vessel he encountered, including English ships, without fear of reprisal from the king. His exploits were rewarded; King John granted him lands in Norfolk and sanctioned his occupation of Sark in the Channel Islands, a strategic base Eustace had captured by force. Eustace's infamy along the southern English coast was such that he needed a safe conduct pass for landing in England, a testament to his feared reputation.

However, the alliance between King John and Eustace began to unravel between 1212 and 1214 AD, a disintegration attributed to multiple factors. A significant strain was King John's alliance with Renaud, the Count of Boulogne and Eustace's long-standing adversary. This alignment deeply aggrieved Eustace. Another potential cause of their falling out was Eustace's failure to repay a debt of 20 marks to the king, resulting in the imprisonment of Eustace and his wife. The "Romance of Eustace" also recounts a harrowing episode where Eustace's daughter, held hostage by John, was brutally mistreated and killed. Additionally, King John, wary of Eustace's growing power, may have perceived him as a threat, culminating in an assault on Eustace's stronghold on Sark.

Reacting to these developments, Eustace shifted his allegiance to the French, serving under King Philip Augustus. Philip, recognizing Eustace's maritime prowess yet aware of his opportunistic nature, is said to have remarked on Eustace's cunning and guile. Eustace was appointed as Philip's admiral, significantly aiding the French cause.

Concurrently, England was engulfed in the First Barons' War, with rebel barons inviting Louis, Philip's son, to claim the English throne from King John. Eustace played a crucial role in the French invasion that began in May 1216, transporting troops and supplies across the Channel. In the spring of the following year, he performed a pivotal act by breaking an English blockade at Rye, rescuing the trapped Prince Louis. Later that year, Eustace's fortunes finally faltered during another rescue operation for Louis.

The French invasion initially saw significant successes, with Louis capturing a substantial portion of England and gaining the support of many English barons. However, the situation shifted after King John's death in October 1216, as the barons began to rally behind Henry III, John's nine-year-old son, as the new English monarch.

The English opposition to Prince Louis intensified, viewing him as an unwelcome invader. In May 1217, Louis' forces suffered a decisive defeat at the Battle of Lincoln, forcing the French into retreat. Despite this setback and initial moves towards peace negotiations, news of impending reinforcements from France emboldened Louis to continue the conflict.

In a critical moment of the First Barons' War, Eustace the Monk played a pivotal role, leading a significant French reinforcement across the English Channel. His fleet, comprising 70 supply ships escorted by 10 warships, faced off against the English forces commanded by Hugh de Burgh. The English, with a fleet of 40 ships, cunningly maneuvered past the French and launched a surprise attack from behind in what became known as the Battle of Sandwich, also referred to as the Battle of Dover. Despite Eustace's leadership and maritime expertise, the French suffered a crushing defeat. The responsibility for this loss, however, fell not on Eustace but on Robert de Courtenay, the future Latin Emperor of Constantinople, who held overall command and thus outranked Eustace.

Hugh de Burgh, realizing the odds were against him in a direct confrontation, cleverly feigned a retreat. Eustace, sensing the trap, warned against pursuit, but his caution was overruled by de Courtenay. The French fleet, losing their advantageous wind position, became vulnerable targets for the smaller, nimble English fleet. The English further outsmarted their adversaries by spreading powdered lime on their decks. Carried by the wind, the lime blinded the French sailors, leading to a decisive English victory and de Courtenay's capture.

Eustace's fate, however, was starkly different. Found hiding in the bilge of his ship, he was captured and offered a substantial ransom for his freedom. But his notorious reputation and the extensive list of atrocities attributed to him made his release impossible. The English, driven by deep-seated animosity, denied him mercy.

Presented with a grim choice for the location of his execution—either at the ship's rail or beside a trebuchet—Eustace faced his end. The historical records do not reveal his choice, but they do name his executioner: Stephan Crabbe. It was Crabbe who ultimately decapitated the infamous pirate, bringing an end to the saga of Eustace the Monk.

The "Romance of Eustace" concludes his story with a poignant moral lesson: "No man can live long who spends his days doing ill." This admonition serves as a somber reflection on the turbulent and morally ambiguous life of Eustace, a figure whose deeds oscillated between daring heroism and ruthless piracy, ultimately sealing his fate in the annals of history.

Jeanne de Clisson

Jeanne de Clisson's life, woven into the fabric of medieval French history, is a tale of nobility, intrigue, and revenge. Born in 1300 into the affluent Belleville family in Belleville-sur-Vie, a picturesque town on France's western coast, Jeanne was renowned for her striking beauty, hailed as one of the most captivating women of her era. Her life took a significant turn when, at the tender age of twelve, she married the nineteen-year-old Geoffrey de Châteaubriant, a union that blessed them with two children before his untimely demise in 1326.

In 1330, Jeanne's path led her to Olivier de Clisson, a man of considerable wealth and nobility. Their marriage, initially more a strategic alliance than a love match, blossomed into a deep, respectful partnership, producing five children. However, their lives were upended by the turbulent War of Breton Succession. Olivier, aligning himself with his boyhood companion Charles de Blois, unwittingly sowed the seeds of his doom. The relationship between Olivier and Charles soured under mysterious circumstances, leading Charles to suspect Olivier of treachery and allegiance to England.

Laura Sook Duncombe, in her illuminating book "Pirate Women," delves into the complexities of this period. She highlights a pivotal moment when the English, after capturing Olivier, demanded a suspiciously modest ransom, fueling Charles's suspicions. Convinced of Olivier's betrayal, Charles and Philip VI, the French King, plotted his downfall.

Their scheme was as cunning as it was cruel. Under the guise of a grand tournament, they lured Olivier and his men into a trap. The group was swiftly arrested and tried for treason. Despite the lack of substantial evidence, Olivier was found guilty and executed, his head gruesomely displayed on a pike in Nantes. This act, both brutal and base, was a shocking deviation from the norms of treating nobility, prompting public outcry. The people of France were largely convinced of Olivier's innocence, viewing the king's actions as a grave miscarriage of justice against a man they believed to be wrongfully condemned.

The tale of Jeanne de Clisson, fueled by grief and a thirst for vengeance, transforms into an epic saga following the tragic execution of her husband. Upon learning of Olivier's brutal fate, Jeanne's world was irrevocably altered. Determined to avenge him, she severed ties with the de Blois family, symbolizing her break from her past life. With her children in tow, she journeyed to Nantes, confronting the gruesome sight of Olivier's severed head. This harrowing moment was not just a personal tragedy but a catalyst for her crusade against those she held responsible.

Stripped of her lands by the king, who deemed them forfeit due to Olivier's supposed treason, Jeanne resorted to liquidating her assets. She sold her jewels, garments, and furniture, gathering funds for her singular mission: to expel the French from Brittany and avenge her husband's unjust death. Her campaign commenced on land, marked by a ferocity that soon became the stuff of legend. Jeanne's strategy was ruthless; she often left just one or two survivors in her wake, ensuring that the tales of her vengeance spread far and wide across France.

However, Jeanne's ambition was not confined to the land. With the remnants of her fortune, she acquired three ships, venturing into a new arena of conflict. The sea became her battleground, and her ferocity remained undiminished. Dubbed the "Lioness of Brittany," her fleet, known as the "Black Fleet," became a symbol of dread. The ships, cloaked in black with sails dyed a menacing red, were a visual testament to her resolve and the impending doom she brought to her enemies. She patrolled the English Channel, relentlessly targeting French vessels, her reputation as a fearsome pirate spreading across Europe.

Yet, despite her fearsome reputation, some saw Jeanne's actions in a different light. Her relentless attacks on French ships undeniably aided the cause of the de Montforts in their claim over Brittany. This led to debates about her true role: was she merely a pirate driven by personal vengeance, or was she an unofficial privateer serving the English cause?

In 1350, even after the death of King Philip VI of France, Jeanne continued her relentless assault on French ships. Her career, which spanned an estimated thirteen years, was marked by piracy and privateering, a rare domain for a woman. Her fierce determination saw her play a pivotal role in the War of Breton Succession, where she was instrumental in keeping Brittany independent of French control. Her actions significantly weakened French troops and their resources, earning her the moniker, 'The Lioness of Brittany.'

The mysteries surrounding her later years are as intriguing as her exploits. After a long career at sea, marked by violence and a ruthless reputation, she surprisingly ended her crusade and married into the English court of Edward III. This decision raises numerous questions. What quenched her thirst for revenge? How did she encounter her new husband amidst her maritime campaigns? The answers to these questions remain elusive.

Historians have little information about Jeanne's final years, except that she died around 1359, five years after her marriage. Her legacy, however, endures. Centuries later, her story continues to captivate, with her and her Black Fleet being remembered as one of the most formidable pirate forces in European history. Jeanne de Clisson, along with other formidable women like Jeanne de Montfort and Jeanne de Penthièvre, carved out a unique space in history, leaving an indelible mark that challenges traditional narratives of women's roles in the Middle Ages.

John Hawley

J ohn Hawley, a figure of near-mythic proportions in the annals of Dartmouth's medieval history, was a man who lived a life of daring contrasts and remarkable achievements. As a wealthy merchant and landowner, he was a titan of commerce. As a politician, he was unrivaled, skillfully navigating the complex waters of local governance to be elected mayor an astounding 14 times and serving twice as Dartmouth's Member of Parliament. But Hawley was not just a man of the land; he was equally masterful at sea. A skilled mariner, he was known for his privateering exploits, heroism in battle, and yes, even piracy.

Born around 1340, John Hawley was a man of many facets, a local hero whose influence in Dartmouth was felt across every street and alleyway, from the bustling marketplace to the quiet corridors of power. His life, spanning the late 14th and early 15th centuries, was a tapestry of daring maritime adventures intertwined with solid civic contributions, making him a pillar of the community.

The origin story of the Hawley family in Dartmouth is a fascinating one. It is believed that the first John Hawley moved to this bustling port town from a small, nearby hamlet called Allaleigh, near Tuckenhay. Some suggest that the name Hawley, occasionally spelled Hauley, might even derive from this quaint locale. During this era, Dartmouth was a town of two halves, split by a tidal inlet that has long since been reclaimed. These two settlements, Hardness to the north and Clifton to the south, were initially distinct entities until their eventual unification in the 13th century by a dam. This dam not only connected the two settlements but also showcased the early ingenuity of Dartmouth's inhabitants in harnessing the power of nature. They utilized the tidal forces to drive a flour mill, a remarkable feat of engineering for the time.

This dam, later known as the Foss, transformed the landscape, creating what was known as the Mill Pool. The name Foss, meaning ditch or moat, hints at the long history of the structure, a history that predates even the Hawley family's arrival in Dartmouth.

By 1344, the Hawleys had begun to make their mark on the town. They constructed a warehouse and set up moorings on the east side of the Foss, near the mill wheel. These moorings, eventually known as Hawley's Hoe, were a testament to the family's burgeoning influence and enterprise. Under the Hawleys' stewardship, a fleet of merchant ships, known as cogs, began to ply the waters, engaging in the lucrative trade of importing wine from France and Spain, and exporting wool from Totnes, a town upstream.

Yet, it wasn't until 1372 that the Hawleys truly came into the public eye, when John, the son of the first John Hawley, emerged as a prominent figure. Historical records from this period are sparse, but it is suggested by some historians, like Edwards, that John may have risen to prominence following the tragic demise of his parents, possibly due to the Black Death, which had ravaged Devon by 1348. By this time, the Hawley fleet had expanded considerably, and their maritime activities had grown in scope and scale, marking a new chapter in the storied history of this influential family.

In 1373, the renowned poet Geoffrey Chaucer, serving as a customs officer for King Edward III, made a significant visit to Dartmouth. His mission was to investigate a controversial incident: the seizure of a Genoese merchant's ship cargo, a matter of delicate importance given the king's amicable ties with Genoa. Although John Hawley wouldn't assume his first mayoral role until 1375, it's widely speculated that Chaucer encountered him during this visit. Many believe that Chaucer's shipman character in his famous works was inspired by Hawley himself. However, as noted by historian Freeman, one should be cautious in directly equating Hawley with Chaucer's fictional character.

Hawley's maritime career took a more adventurous turn in 1379, during his third term as mayor, when he received his first privateer license. This period marked an escalation in the ongoing war with France, and it was then that Hawley's actions began to tread the line between heroism and infamy.

Chaucer's depiction of his shipman character is intriguing, portraying him as a skilled navigator who harbored a more sinister side. The character was known for craftily stealing wine from cargoes and coldly disposing of captured sailors at sea.

The strategic significance of Dartmouth as a port was well-recognized, prompting Edward III to order special defensive measures in 1374. However, it wasn't until 1388, under Richard II's reign, that John Hawley, serving yet again as mayor, initiated the construction of a fortalice, or coastal fort, at Dartmouth's harbor entrance. This move underscored the growing importance and vulnerability of Dartmouth in the face of maritime threats.

By 1400, the fortalice at Dartmouth, a vital piece of defensive architecture, was completed. Notably, a chain was installed across the river to Godmerock, which could be raised to block enemy ships from entering Dartmouth. This fortalice was an early precursor to the now-famous Dartmouth Castle, whose construction began much later in 1481 during Edward IV's reign. Across the harbor mouth, Kingswear Castle began its construction in 1491. Today, the remnants of the original fortalice might not be immediately evident, but a closer examination, as pointed out by historian Edwards, reveals traces of its existence, such as the high wall with a tower above the car park and other subtle clues scattered around the site.

The existing Dartmouth Castle, features a round tower and a glimpse of a square tower in the background, with part of St Petrox Church visible in the right foreground. Edwards' analysis suggests that this round tower may have been built atop an older structure, possibly part of the original fortalice. This hypothesis is supported by the noticeable differences in masonry, especially evident near the wide opening for the chain's cable when viewed from the rocks below.

During John Hawley's lifetime, England and France were embroiled in the protracted conflict known later as the Hundred Years' War, mainly centered around English claims to the French throne. In this era, kings lacked a standing navy and instead issued privateering licenses to merchant ship owners. These licenses permitted them to use their ships to attack and destroy the king's enemies at their own expense.

For merchants like John Hawley, who commanded a disciplined and well-armed fleet, privateering was not only a patriotic duty but also a lucrative venture. The king would claim a share of the value of seized enemy cargoes, while the rest was distributed among the ship owners, captains, and their courageous crews. However, the temptation to engage in piracy against nations not at war with the king was ever-present. Such actions, while technically piracy, were difficult to police, especially considering that maritime piracy remains a challenge even in the 21st century.

Disputes often arose when neutral ships were captured, as in the case of Chaucer's Genoese merchant, or when goods belonging to a neutral third party were found on an enemy vessel. In such cases, the aggrieved merchant could demand the return of their property, often leading to protracted legal battles in English courts. The accused would typically argue that they had acted within the bounds of the law, prolonging these legal disputes.

The event in 1384, where John Hawley was ambushed and held for ransom in a Brittany port, might have fueled his later maritime ventures. In 1386,

Hawley and Sir John de Roches, then captain of Brest (an English stronghold), were likely allies in various operations. However, a dispute over spoils led to a falling out, and in 1393, Roches accused Hawley in the Court of Chivalry of seizing Breton vessels under his protection. The allegations against Hawley were not of direct involvement in the capture, but rather of approving the robbery by distributing and keeping a portion of the loot.

It appears Hawley wasn't personally engaged in many such incidents; he relied on his ship-masters to follow naval warfare rules and protect their shares of any gains. When the trial ensued, many of Hawley's seamen testified, some via special commissioners in Dartmouth to avoid travel to London. Countercharges were brought against Roches, and the proceedings were temporarily halted, arguing that maritime disputes belonged in the Admiralty Court. The final outcome is unclear, but Hawley's reputation seemingly remained intact, with the case concluding around 1401 after Roches' death.

In 1403, Hawley's raids on Flemish and Dutch ships led to retaliatory actions by the Count of Flanders. Summoned by the king to answer for these actions, Hawley and other privateers did not appear. Before further royal intervention, the West Country faced a dramatic event. William du Chatel, the Breton leader, retaliated by raiding Plymouth in 1403, prompting the king to commission Dartmouth's leading seamen, including Hawley, for a counter-offensive.

Anticipating a Breton attack, Dartmouth prepared for an incursion in April 1404. However, du Chatel landed at Blackpool Sands near Slapton, attempting a surprise attack. Hawley, stationed at the fortalice, sent forces to confront the Bretons. Freeman describes the battle: Du Chatel's forces, weakened by desertions and lacking crossbowmen, faced a fortified English position. Despite being taunted for hesitance, du Chatel attacked but faced heavy casualties. Many knights perished, some drowning due to their armor's weight. Women and peasants reportedly fought alongside English soldiers. The battle culminated in du Chatel's mortal wounding, capture of several high-ranking prisoners, and a retreat by the remaining Breton forces.

This unexpected victory by a makeshift army so impressed King Henry that he celebrated with a Te Deum in Westminster Abbey.

King Henry IV's initial approval of John Hawley's military successes soon faded. By 1405, Hawley had returned to privateering, often attacking groups aligned with Henry IV, who was threatening to arrest seamen for illegitimately seizing goods. This behavior led to Hawley's brief incarceration in the Tower of London in December 1406, until he agreed to compensate Barcelona merchants and secured a £3000 surety from his West Country allies. Remarkably, even at 68, Hawley was implicated in the illegal seizure of 17 ships.

Hawley, who held significant prestige as a Crown agent in Devon and as a defender of the southwestern peninsula, often ignored the King's orders to compensate foreign merchants for the cargoes he had seized. The Crown's reliance on figures like Hawley during foreign threats highlighted their importance to the monarchy, a fact they exploited to continue their high-seas activities.

In 2008, the six-hundredth anniversary of Hawley's death led to a reassessment of his legacy. A contemporary West Country privateer, Harry Pay of Poole, Dorset, shared Hawley's reputation for bold actions and service to the king. Kingsford views both Pay and Hawley as overall positive figures, despite the apparent contradictions in their actions and loyalties, characterizing them as patriots who occasionally veered into piracy.

In Hawley's time, coastal towns like Dartmouth often had to defend their shipping and shores independently, leading to necessary but sometimes dubious actions. Hawley's wealth, deeply connected to maritime trade, drove him to keep sea routes open by any means. This economic imperative often led to actions that were essential for survival in a period marked by frequent maritime conflicts.

John Hawley's life as a privateer and pirate epitomizes the complex and often ambiguous nature of naval warfare during his era. His controversial actions were part of a broader context of survival and economic interest in a time of widespread turbulence and conflict.

St. Saviour's Church in Dartmouth, a magnificent example of medieval architecture, was consecrated in 1372. It boasts an impressive rood-screen and a painted stone pulpit that both date back to this period.

John Hawley, a prominent figure in Dartmouth, was responsible for the construction of St. Saviour's chancel. Upon his death in 1408, his tomb was placed there. The tomb features a brass portrait of Hawley in armor, flanked by his two wives, each adorned with jeweled hair and accompanied by small dogs with bell-collared collars. John outlived both wives: Joanna, who passed away in 1394, and Alicia, who died in 1403. His son, also named John, followed in his father's footsteps as a privateer and was similarly accused of piracy multiple times.

John Hawley Junior continued to manage the family's business interests in merchant trading and landownership. He also served multiple terms as the Member of Parliament for Dartmouth. His death in 1436 marked the end of the influential Hawley era in Dartmouth, especially since his own son Nicholas died childless a few years later. The Hawley fortune, which included properties in Cornwall and Dartmouth, was then inherited by Nicholas' sister Elizabeth, who was married to John Copleston.

The Coplestons and their descendants lived in the Hawleys' house until 1494, when it was sold to the burgesses. The house then served as the Guildhall until 1864, when it was demolished during a road expansion project to improve access to the town.

John Crabbe

John Crabbe, hailing from the quaint town of Muide in Flanders (now known as Sint Anna ter Muiden in the Dutch province of Zeeland), grew up in a locale steeped in maritime heritage. Nestled on the coast near the Zwin river mouth, this region was a bustling maritime hub in the fourteenth century, linking the North Sea with the thriving cities of Bruges, Damme, and Sluis. Crabbe may have shared familial ties with Peter and Baldwin Crabbe, speculated to be his brothers, and was known to have a nephew affectionately named Crabbekin.

Crabbe's piratical escapades first came into the limelight in 1305. His audacious attack on the Waardeboure of Dordrecht at La Rochelle in the Bay of Biscay marked the beginning of his notorious career. In this daring raid, Crabbe seized a substantial cargo of 160 tuns of wine, torched the vessel, and took the sailors hostage. William Gurstelle attributes Crabbe's success in this venture to his innovative use of a deck-mounted catapult. Given that Dordrecht fell under John II, Count of Holland's jurisdiction, and considering the longstanding animosity between Holland, Zeeland, and Flanders, Crabbe likely viewed the Waardeboure as fair game. The ship's owner, a Dordrecht merchant named John de le Waerde, sought a hefty compensation of 2,000 livres tournois, even enlisting King Philip IV of France's aid. However, despite ongoing efforts and legal proceedings, Crabbe and his crew eluded retribution.

Crabbe's trail went cold until 1310 when he resurfaced with the capture of a lavishly laden ship belonging to Alice of Hainault, Countess Marshal. The vessel, brimming with cloth, jewels, and precious metals, was en route to London via the Strait of Dover. Edward II of England's attempts to bring Crabbe to justice were in vain, and in 1315, only Crabbe's men faced punishment. To compensate the countess, Edward II ordered the confiscation of Flemish assets in London.

By this period, Crabbe had seemingly settled in Aberdeen, Scotland, where he possibly had relatives. In Aberdeen, he was embroiled in disputes over land rights in Cults, Cromar. Over time, the Crabbe family name evolved into Craib, and by the 1700s, the Craibs were established as farmers in Strathmore, Cromar. Lucas notes that Flemish merchants were welcomed in Scotland, especially given the ongoing hostilities with England. This acceptance allowed them to prey on English merchant ships, funneling the spoils back to Flanders.

In 1311, Crabbe's reach extended to seizing two Newcastle-on-Tyne merchant ships headed to Flanders, loaded with eighty-nine sacks of wool. Crabbe's allies in Aberdeen assisted in transporting the wool to Flanders for sale. Despite the Newcastle merchants' protests to Edward II, Crabbe's piratical activities continued unchecked, further fueling the tense maritime politics of the era.

In the years following 1316, John Crabbe's whereabouts and actions remain shrouded in mystery. However, a severe famine struck Flanders in 1316, prompting Count Robert to summon Crabbe back from his obscure sojourns. Recognizing his maritime prowess, the Count entrusted Crabbe with the crucial role of admiral, commanding a fleet tasked with the dire mission of securing food to mitigate the famine's effects. In fulfilling this mandate, Crabbe captured two ships from Great Yarmouth merchants.

December of that same year witnessed another of Crabbe's notable exploits. He intercepted La Bona Navis de la Strode near the Isle of Thanet, seizing its valuable cargo of wine destined for the English market. This act of piracy drew the attention of the English king, who over the next five years repeatedly pressed Count Robert for action against Crabbe. Count Robert, in a letter dated 14 November 1317, distanced himself from Crabbe, claiming ignorance of his location and stating that Crabbe, accused of murder, had been exiled and would face harsh punishment if found.

Crabbe's reputation as a feared pirate was now firmly established, even catching the attention of Lodewijk van Velthem, an Antwerp chronicler. Crabbe returned to Scotland, taking up residence in Berwick where he acquired the status of a burgess. Despite this apparent settlement, he continued his assaults on English vessels.

His notoriety extended to the battlegrounds. During the English siege of Berwick in 1318–1319, Crabbe played a significant role in the town's defense. His contributions were immortalized in verse by John Barbour, author of "The Bruce," highlighting Crabbe's cunning and strategic acumen.

The year 1332 marked a new chapter in the ongoing conflicts between England and Scotland. Edward III of England supported Edward Balliol's claim to the Scottish throne, leading to the Scots' defeat at the Battle of Dupplin Moor. Crabbe, commanding a fleet of ten Flemish ships, suffered a decisive defeat at the hands of the English in the Firth of Tay. Following this setback, Crabbe retreated to Berwick but was soon captured by English soldier Walter de Manny.

An English Parliament convened in York then played a crucial role in Crabbe's fate. They petitioned Edward III, allowing Manny a substantial ransom of 4,300 marks from the Scots for Crabbe's release. However, Edward III ordered that Crabbe remain imprisoned and in chains in Scotland until he compensated for the robbery of the Bona Navis.

Crabbe, fearing his English captors, managed to persuade John Randolph, 3rd Earl of Moray, to secure a safe conduct for him to the English court until Michaelmas 1333. Upon his arrival in England, Edward III decided to detain

Crabbe, compensating Manny with 1,000 marks for the ransom.

The siege of Berwick resumed in the spring of 1333. Following the Scots' defeat at the Battle of Halidon Hill on 19 July 1333, they refused to ransom Crabbe, partly due to reports from the Lanercost Chronicle that he had aided Edward III during the siege. Tragically, this led to the execution of Crabbe's son by the Scots. In a surprising turn of events, Edward III, acknowledging Crabbe's service during the siege of Berwick, granted him a full pardon for all his crimes, both on land and sea, and appointed him as the Constable of Somerton Castle, marking a dramatic transformation in Crabbe's life from a notorious pirate to a recognized and rewarded figure under the English crown.

In the years following his appointment as Constable of Somerton Castle, John Crabbe emerged as a pivotal figure in Edward III's military campaigns, particularly during the ongoing hostilities with Scotland. His contributions to the English war efforts were multifaceted and significant.

Between February and March 1335, Crabbe undertook a notable maritime endeavor. He assembled a formidable fleet of ten ships from various English ports, ensuring they were well-provisioned and manned. These vessels were then deployed at sea under the king's command, bolstering England's naval presence in the conflict with Scotland.

Crabbe's expertise was not limited to naval engagements. He also played a key role in strengthening ground defenses. His efforts in reinforcing the fortifications at Berwick underscored his strategic importance in land-based military operations. Additionally, in 1338, Crabbe's talents were further showcased when he was instrumental in the construction of engines and hoardings for the siege of Dunbar Castle. These feats of military engineering demonstrated his versatility and ingenuity in warfare. For these services, he received due compensation from the crown and was held in high esteem, as reflected in contemporary documents that referred to him as the king's yeoman and, on one occasion, as the king's sergeant.

The onset of the Hundred Years' War in 1337 brought a new dimension to Crabbe's role in Edward III's strategic plans. With the war's epicenter shifting to the Low Countries, Edward III aimed to utilize this region as a base for military operations while financing the war through the sale of English wool. The safe passage of English shipping, particularly for wool trade, became a paramount concern. Crabbe, with his naval prowess and familiarity with the sea routes, was ideally suited to assist in this endeavor.

From 4 April to 12 August 1339, Crabbe's naval responsibilities reached a new peak. He served alongside Robert de Morley, 2nd Baron Morley, the Admiral of the Fleet North of the Thames. During this time, Crabbe displayed remarkable leadership and tactical skills. He commanded a contingent of a hundred archers, showcasing his ability to lead and manage large groups of combatants effectively. On another occasion, he led a diverse force comprising eight men-at-arms, seventy archers, and seventy sailors, further demonstrating his adeptness in leading mixed military units. This period of service not only highlights Crabbe's central role in maintaining the security of key maritime routes but also underscores his importance in Edward III's broader military strategy during the early phases of the Hundred Years' War.

In a strategic move to counteract the English use of the Low Countries as a military base, Philip VI of France mustered a formidable fleet at the mouths of the Zwin and Scheldt rivers. In response, Edward III of England, ready for immediate action, convened a crucial council meeting at Orwell. Prominent figures such as John de Stratford, the Archbishop of Canterbury, Lord Morley, and John Crabbe were in attendance. During this assembly, the trio, recognizing the gravity of the situation, counseled the king to delay his attack until a larger, more robust fleet could be assembled. Edward III, though hesitant, acquiesced to their advice.

This strategic decision culminated in the momentous Battle of Sluys on 23 June. The English fleet, now significantly reinforced, clashed with the French in a fierce naval engagement that lasted the entire afternoon. By day's end, the English forces had almost completely decimated the French fleet. However, a few French vessels, under the command of a pirate named Spoudevisch, managed to slip away. Edward III, determined to leave no enemy unchallenged, ordered Crabbe to pursue these remnants. The historical records, however, remain silent on whether Crabbe succeeded in this mission. Following the victory at Sluys, Crabbe possibly accompanied the king to the siege of Tournai, although specific details of his involvement in this siege are not well-documented.

The prolonged war with France severely strained Edward III's finances. In a move to alleviate this fiscal crisis, the grant previously awarded to Crabbe in 1333 was revoked on 10 October 1341. In its stead, Crabbe received the custody and profits of Somerton Castle, a significant and strategic asset. Despite these changes, Crabbe continued to be a valuable asset to the king. In early 1341, he supplied timber for the construction of military "engines" at the king's manor of Langley Marsh in Buckinghamshire. He also played a role in fortifying Fauxhall with barricades. By December of the same year, Crabbe's responsibilities expanded to include aiding in the replenishment of the royal treasury, as he was tasked with the collection of certain dues in Nottinghamshire.

Crabbe's service extended beyond fiscal and construction contributions. After the English victory at the Battle of Neville's Cross on 17 October 1346, Edward III prohibited the ransom of Scottish prisoners. Instead, these captives were distributed across various castles for safekeeping. In August 1347, Crabbe was summoned by the council in this regard. He was entrusted with the custody of Walter de Maundeville, who had been previously imprisoned in the Tower of London. This assignment not only illustrates Crabbe's continued importance in the realm's affairs but also his involvement in the broader geopolitical strategies of Edward III's reign.

John Crabbe's eventful and impactful life came to an end in early 1352. His death marked the conclusion of a career that had seen him transition from a notorious pirate to a respected military commander and a trusted royal servant, playing a pivotal role in some of the most significant naval and military episodes of Edward III's reign.

Klaus Störtebeker

Klaus Störtebeker, born in 1360 in Wismar, a North German town, is shrouded in mystery, with only sparse details about his early life. A notable incident in 1380 marked his name in the annals of history: two men, one named Nicolao Störtebeker, were expelled from Wismar following a violent brawl, an event emblematic of Störtebeker's rebellious nature. His moniker, Störtebeker, meaning 'down the beakerful' in German, is a testament to his legendary drinking prowess, famously capable of consuming a 4-liter mug of beer in a single gulp. Beyond his drinking feats, Störtebeker was a notorious pirate. From 1389, he led the "Vitalien Brothers," a group of rapacious pirates, causing chaos across the Baltic Sea for over a decade.

Störtebeker ascended to leadership of the Victual Brothers, a ruthless band of privateers who terrorized the Baltic during the 1390s. The earliest records of the Victual Brothers date back to 1389 when the town council of Dorpat reacted to a complaint from Reval about them selling ships to "de vitalien-brude." Their reputation was already formidable, viewed as untrustworthy mercenaries and feared pirates. In 1390, the Hamburg Chamber of Finance recorded dispatching an armada to combat the "Vitalienses."

Störtebeker's tenure with the German royal house of Mecklenburg is the best-documented phase of his life. The Danish and Swedish thrones were contested after the death of Waldemar IV Atterdag, King of Denmark (1321-1375). The struggle was between Queen Margaret of Norway, Waldemar's daughter, and

Albrecht III, King of Sweden and son of the Duke of Mecklenburg. Albrecht III, leveraging his seaports at Wismar and Rostock, began recruiting privateers to attack Danish ships in the Baltic, aiming to weaken Queen Margaret's claim to the throne. Störtebeker, renowned for his maritime prowess, found his place in this tumultuous period, shaping his legacy as a feared and legendary figure of the Baltic seas.

In the year 1392, Klaus Störtebeker, already a feared figure in the Baltic Sea, and his band of pirates, the Victual Brothers, were recruited by the Germans during one of their strategic hiring drives. The Germans, embroiled in a maritime conflict, recognized the potential of Störtebeker's ruthless efficiency and maritime expertise. The pirates' first significant assignment under this new allegiance occurred in 1394, tasked with the critical mission of supplying the besieged city of Stockholm with vital resources. It was during this mission that they earned the moniker "Victual Brothers," a name derived from the Latin word 'victualia,' signifying foodstuffs or provisions, highlighting their role in transporting essential supplies.

The impact of Störtebeker and his men on the Baltic maritime landscape was profound. In 1395, Franciscan friar Detmar chronicled their exploits, painting a vivid picture of the chaos they wrought upon the sea. His writings detailed how the Victual Brothers had not only disrupted maritime trade and travel but were also known for their indiscriminate attacks, including on erstwhile allies.

This tumult had far-reaching consequences. Reports from Magdeburg and Limburg in the same period noted a significant hike in the price of salt-herring, a staple in the diets of the common folk, a direct result of the Victual Brothers' blockade of Scania.

However, the political landscape shifted in 1395 with a peace treaty that saw Albrecht relinquishing control over Sweden and Denmark to Queen Margaret. But this change in political fortunes did little to alter Störtebeker's course.

Accustomed to the lure of plunder and the chaos of piracy, he and his men continued their reign of terror on the Baltic Sea, indifferent to the changing political allegiances. By 1397, as Queen Margaret solidified her reign over the Danish and Swedish thrones and formed the Kalmar Union, Störtebeker's infamy continued to grow, his actions contributing to the volatile atmosphere of the high seas.

During this era, the Baltic Sea's trade was dominated by the Hanseatic League, a powerful alliance of North German states, overseeing the movement of vast quantities of gold and goods from key ports like Hamburg, Lübeck, and Rostock. Sensing an opportunity in this wealth of maritime commerce, Störtebeker established a base on the island of Gotland. Here, he transformed Visby, the island's largest town, into a veritable pirate stronghold. His reign of piracy was marked by several years of successful raids and interceptions.

However, in 1398, the tide began to turn against Störtebeker and his crew. The island of Gotland faced an invasion by the knights of the Teutonic Order, who effectively expelled Störtebeker's pirates from their Baltic stronghold. Forced to flee, they sought refuge along the rugged coastlines of the North Sea, finding allies in the Frisians of modern-day Holland. Adapting to their new environment, the pirates began targeting the lucrative shipping lanes to England and the English Channel.

The final chapter of Klaus Störtebeker's notorious career unfolded over the span of four additional years, filled with successful yet increasingly perilous endeavors. By 1401, the cities of Hamburg and Lübeck, weary of Störtebeker's relentless piracy, mounted a determined offensive. They dispatched a formidable flotilla, commanded by the skilled captain Simon of Utrecht, specifically to target the pirate stronghold in Frisia. This decisive move marked the beginning of the end for Störtebeker and his band of corsairs.

The Hamburg englandfahrer company, renowned for their maritime prowess, eventually succeeded in capturing Störtebeker and his crew. However, Gödeke

Michels, Störtebeker's faithful co-pirate, initially eluded capture. His freedom was short-lived, as he was later cornered and killed in a dramatic stand-off on the Jade, a river delta in the Weser region, a year after Störtebeker's capture.

The circumstances surrounding Störtebeker's capture were shrouded in treachery. It was alleged that one of his own crewmembers, in a stunning act of betrayal, had sabotaged their ship by pouring molten lead on the chains controlling the ship's rudder, rendering it immobile and vulnerable to capture.

Following their capture, Störtebeker and his cohorts were transported to Heligoland and then to Hamburg aboard the frigate "Bunte Kuh" or "Motley Cow." In Hamburg, they awaited their fate. In a desperate bid for freedom, Störtebeker offered the city officials a lavish bribe: a gold chain long enough to encircle the entire city of Hamburg. The wealth he had amassed from his numerous raids was indeed substantial; it is said that the gold confiscated from his ship later financed the construction of the tip of St. Catherine's Cathedral in Hamburg. Despite this tempting offer, the authorities remained resolute, sentencing Störtebeker and seventy of his crew to death by beheading.

The execution of Klaus Störtebeker, carried out on October 20th on the island of Grasbrook on the Elbe River, was an event of extraordinary and macabre spectacle. Störtebeker, facing his imminent demise, negotiated a bizarre agreement with the executioner and Hamburg's city councilors. They consented to a chilling wager: after Störtebeker's decapitation, his headless body would be allowed to walk past his imprisoned crewmates, and every man he passed would be granted freedom. Incredibly, after the executioner struck, Störtebeker's body managed to stagger past 11 of his men before being deliberately tripped. However, the authorities reneged on their promise, and all of Störtebeker's fellow pirates were summarily executed.

The aftermath of this brutal spectacle saw the heads of Störtebeker and his crew impaled on spikes along the Hamburg city walls, serving as a gruesome warning to any aspiring pirates. This marked the end of Störtebeker's reign, sealing his legacy as one of the most feared and legendary figures in the annals of piracy.

The story of Klaus Störtebeker, already rich in drama and intrigue, is further embellished by a rather ironic and darkly humorous epilogue concerning his execution. After the mass execution of Störtebeker and his crew, a curious and somewhat grim exchange reportedly took place between the city councilors of Hamburg and the executioner. When inquired if the task of beheading so many had exhausted him, the executioner, perhaps in a macabre attempt at humor, claimed his arms were still strong enough to behead the entire council. This jest, unsurprisingly, was not well-received by the councilors, and in a swift turn of events, the executioner himself was sentenced to death. Adding to the irony, his execution was carried out by the youngest member of the city council.

This tale took a fascinating archaeological turn centuries later. In 1878, a skull with a spike through it was discovered at Grasbrook, the very site of Störtebeker's execution. Believed to be Störtebeker's – whose head was said to have been displayed on a spike – this skull was later exhibited in the Museum for Hamburg History in 1922, symbolizing a tangible connection to the legendary pirate. The mystery deepened in 2008 when scientists attempted to verify the skull's identity by comparing DNA samples from the skull with those of Störtebeker's potential living descendants. Although the results were inconclusive, the skull continues to be associated with Störtebeker and is a prized exhibit at the museum, accompanied by a digital facial reconstruction of the notorious raider.

Störtebeker's legacy has transcended the boundaries of mere historical figure to become a folk hero in German culture. He is often romanticized as a Robin Hood-like figure, a bandit with a heart, who redistributed his ill-gotten gains among the poor. This aspect of his legend is further enhanced by references to his crew as 'likedeelers', a term suggesting their commitment to sharing plunder equally among themselves. Störtebeker's story, interwoven with elements of rebellion, bravado, and a touch of benevolence, continues to captivate the imagination, making him an enduring figure in the annals of folklore and history.

Oruç Reis

Oruç Reis, a prominent figure in Ottoman history, stands tall as a legendary corsair who eventually rose to become the Sultan of Algiers. Born around 1474 on the Ottoman-controlled island of Midilli (now known as Lesbos in modern-day Greece), his life was a tapestry of daring exploits and naval mastery, culminating in his death in a fierce battle against the Spanish at Tlemcen in 1518. The elder brother of the renowned Ottoman admiral Hayreddin Barbarossa, Oruç's legacy is intertwined with pivotal moments of Mediterranean history.

Oruç gained the affectionate moniker of Baba Oruç (Father Oruç) for his heroic role in rescuing and transporting large numbers of Morisco, Muslim, and Jewish refugees from Spain to the safer havens of North Africa. This act of mercy and defiance against the backdrop of religious persecution in Europe led to his name being transformed in European folklore to Barbarossa, which translates to 'Redbeard' in Italian, a testament to his imposing presence and fiery spirit.

His father, Yakup Ağa, was an influential Ottoman official of either Turkish or Albanian descent. Yakup Ağa played a significant role in the Ottoman conquest of Lesbos from the Genoese in 1462. As a reward for his valor and service, he was granted the fiefdom of the Bonova village on the island. He married Katerina, a local Christian Greek woman and the widow of an Eastern Orthodox priest, blending cultures and religions in their family.

Yakup Ağa and Katerina had six children – two daughters and four sons: Ishak, Oruç, Hızır (who later became known as Hayreddin Barbarossa), and Ilyas. Yakup, a skilled potter, also owned a boat to trade his products across the seas. The family business was a collective effort, with the sons contributing to different aspects of the trade. Oruç initially assisted with the boat, a role that likely ignited his passion for the sea, while Hızır lent his hands to the pottery business.

Oruç Reis's journey from a humble assistant in his father's trade to a revered leader and feared corsair is a tale of resilience, strategic acumen, and a relentless pursuit of sovereignty and safety for those persecuted. His life, marked by dramatic battles, strategic alliances, and a legendary escape from captivity, carved a permanent place for him in the annals of Mediterranean maritime history.

The Reis brothers, Ishak, Oruç, Hızır, and Ilyas, each carved their distinct paths on the tumultuous seas of the Mediterranean, intertwining their destinies with the era's maritime and mercantile adventures. Oruç, the most adventurous of the siblings, was the first to venture into seamanship, with his youngest brother Ilyas soon following in his wake. Hızır, initially involved in their father's pottery business, later acquired his own ship and embarked on a maritime career. Ishak, the eldest, chose a different route, staying on Mytilene to manage the family's financial affairs.

Their journey at sea began as sailors, but the brothers soon found themselves drawn into the more perilous and adrenaline-fueled world of privateering. They were particularly focused on counteracting the activities of the Knights Hospitaller based in Rhodes, a formidable and influential military order known for its naval prowess.

Oruç and Ilyas initially focused their efforts in the Levant, navigating the waters between Anatolia, Syria, and Egypt. Hızır, on the other hand, operated predominantly in the Aegean Sea, with Thessaloniki serving as his base of operations. These early experiences not only honed their skills in navigation and combat but also exposed them to diverse cultures and languages. Oruç, in particular, became a polyglot, mastering Italian, Spanish, French, Greek, and Arabic, skills that would greatly aid his later ventures.

His seafaring career, marked by success and daring, took a dramatic turn during a trading expedition in Tripoli, Lebanon. He and Ilyas were ambushed by a galley belonging to the Knights Hospitaller. The encounter was brutal; Ilyas lost his life, and Oruç sustained serious injuries. This battle also resulted in the loss of their father's boat and Oruç's capture, leading to his imprisonment in the Knights' formidable Bodrum Castle.

Oruç's time in captivity was harrowing. Initially subjected to torture, he was later forced into slavery, toiling on a Rhodes ship that transported prisoners. However, his resilience and determination shone through even in these dark times. One night, under favorable conditions, Oruç managed a daring escape from the ship. He found refuge in a village, where he spent ten days recuperating and planning his next move. This period of his life was not just a test of his endurance but also a catalyst for his later exploits. Eventually, Oruç joined forces with Captain Ali, a decision that marked the beginning of a new chapter in his life.

Oruç Reis, following his escape and subsequent adventures, eventually made his way to Antalya. There, he caught the attention of Şehzade Korkut, an Ottoman prince and the governor of the city. Recognizing Oruç's naval prowess, Şehzade Korkut entrusted him with a formidable fleet of 18 galleys. His mission was clear: to combat the Knights Hospitaller, who were causing significant disruption to Ottoman maritime trade and shipping routes.

Armed with his new fleet, embarked on a series of naval campaigns that significantly bolstered his reputation as a skilled mariner and tactician. When Şehzade Korkut became the governor of Manisa, he further expanded Oruç's fleet, granting him 24 galleys at the port of İzmir. This larger fleet enabled

Oruç to participate in an ambitious Ottoman naval expedition to Apulia in the Kingdom of Naples. In this campaign, Oruç demonstrated his military acumen by bombarding coastal forts and capturing enemy ships. On his return journey to Lesbos, he made a strategic stop at Euboea, where he seized three galleons and another ship.

His campaign against the Knights Hospitaller continued with increased intensity. He launched attacks on several of their islands, capturing numerous vessels. Upon returning to Mytilene with his captured ships, he received troubling news. Şehzade Korkut, now a brother of the new Ottoman sultan, had fled to Egypt to escape potential assassination—a common occurrence in the Ottoman succession struggles. Concerned about potential repercussions due to his close ties with the exiled prince, Oruç set sail for Egypt. In Cairo, he managed to secure an audience with the Mamluk Sultan Qansuh al-Ghawri. The Sultan, recognizing Oruç's naval capabilities, provided him with another ship and tasked him with raiding the coasts of Italy and other Christian-controlled Mediterranean islands.

After spending the winter in Cairo, Oruç embarked on his new mission from Alexandria. He successfully operated along the Ligurian and Sicilian coasts, further enhancing his reputation as a formidable corsair. In 1503, he expanded his fleet with three more ships and established Djerba, an island in the Western Mediterranean, as his new base of operations. It was here that Hızır, Oruç's brother, joined him.

In 1504, Oruç and Hızır approached Abu Abdallah Muhammad IV al-Mutawakkil, the Hafsid caliph of Tunisia, seeking permission to use the port of La Goulette for their operations. The caliph granted this request, with the condition that one-third of their booty be given to him. Operating from La Goulette, Oruç commanded small galliots and successfully captured two larger Papal galleys near Elba. Near Lipari, the brothers seized a significant Sicilian warship, the Cavalleria, carrying Spanish soldiers and knights, further bolstering their fleet and fame.

In the subsequent years, Oruç and his brothers continued their successful raids along the Italian coast, particularly targeting the coasts of Liguria and Calabria. Their growing renown attracted other notable Muslim corsairs, including Kurtoğlu (Curtogoli in the West), a Turkish corsair from Kayseri. Their exploits were not just about plunder; they had a significant impact on the power dynamics of the Mediterranean.

In 1509, Ishak, the eldest brother, also left Mytilene to join Oruç and Hızır at La Goulette. Between 1504 and 1510, Oruç's humanitarian efforts in transporting Muslims from Spain to North Africa earned him widespread admiration and the honorific name Baba Oruç (Father Oruç). This deed, marked by compassion and leadership, further cemented his legacy. In Spain, Italy, and France, due to the phonetic similarity, Baba Oruç's name gradually evolved into Barbarossa (Redbeard in Italian), a moniker that would become synonymous with his legendary status as a master corsair and protector of the oppressed.

The year 1510 marked a significant escalation in the maritime exploits of the three Reis brothers. They launched a daring raid on Cape Passero in Sicily and successfully repelled a Spanish assault on Bougie, Oran, and Algiers. Their naval prowess continued to grow, and in August 1511, they extended their raids to the regions around Reggio Calabria in southern Italy, demonstrating their capacity to strike deep into enemy territories.

August 1512 brought a turning point in Oruç Reis's career. The exiled ruler of Bougie sought the brothers' assistance to expel the Spaniards. In the fierce battle that ensued, Oruç suffered a grievous injury, losing his left arm. This event led to his being known as Gümüş Kol, meaning 'Silver Arm' in Turkish, a reference to the silver prosthetic device he used thereafter. Undeterred by this setback, the brothers continued their maritime campaigns. Later in 1512, they raided the coasts of Andalusia in Spain, capturing a galliot owned by the Genoese Lomellini family, who had holdings in Tabarca. Their campaign extended to Menorca, where they seized a coastal castle, followed by a bold assault near Liguria, capturing four Genoese galleys. Even when the

Genoese dispatched a fleet for recovery, the brothers triumphed, capturing their flagship as well. In a remarkable feat, they amassed 23 ships in less than a month, before returning to their base at La Goulette.

At La Goulette, their naval strength was further bolstered by the construction of three more galliots and a facility for gunpowder production. In 1513, their operations expanded to capturing four English ships en route to France, followed by a raid on Valencia, capturing four more ships. Their campaign then took them to Alicante, where they seized a Spanish galley near Málaga.

Between 1513 and 1514, the Reis brothers frequently engaged Spanish squadrons, eventually moving to a new base in Cherchell, west of Algiers. In 1514, with a formidable fleet of 12 galliots and 1,000 Turks, they obliterated two Spanish fortresses at Bougie. When a Spanish fleet under Miguel de Gurrea, viceroy of Majorca, arrived for assistance, the brothers audaciously moved towards Ceuta, raiding the city before capturing Jijel in Algeria, which was under Genoese control. Their relentless campaigns continued with the capture of Mahdiya in Tunisia, followed by raids along the coasts of Sicily, Sardinia, the Balearic Islands, and the Spanish mainland, where they captured three large ships.

The year 1515 saw them seizing several galleons, a galley, and three barques at Majorca. In a significant diplomatic move, Oruç sent lavish gifts to the Ottoman Sultan Selim I, who reciprocated with two galleys and two diamond-embellished swords. In 1516, alongside Kurtoğlu, another renowned corsair, the brothers laid siege to the Castle of Elba and later returned to Liguria, capturing 12 ships and inflicting damage on 28 others.

These years were marked by a series of audacious naval victories and strategic expansions, solidifying the Reis brothers, particularly Oruç, as formidable powers in the Mediterranean. Their ability to commandeer ships, capture strategic locations, and engage effectively against larger naval forces spoke volumes of their tactical genius and fearless approach to maritime warfare.

The year 1516 marked a pivotal moment in the careers of the three Reis brothers, Oruç, Hızır, and Ilyas, as they embarked on a significant campaign that would change the political landscape of North Africa. They successfully liberated Jijel and Algiers from Spanish control, a feat that demonstrated their growing military prowess. However, instead of simply freeing these cities, the brothers assumed control over them and the surrounding region, effectively displacing the previous ruler, Abu Hammu Musa III of the Zayyanid dynasty, who was compelled to flee.

This takeover had immediate repercussions. The local Spanish population in Algiers, finding themselves under new and unexpected rulers, took refuge in the Peñón of Algiers. In a desperate plea for aid, they appealed to Emperor Charles V, the King of Spain, to intervene. However, even the involvement of the Spanish fleet was not enough to dislodge the Reis brothers from their newfound stronghold in Algiers.

Following the consolidation of his rule in Algiers, Oruç declared himself the new Sultan of Algiers and swiftly turned his attention to expanding his territory inland. He led successful campaigns to capture Miliana, Medea, and Ténès, showcasing not only his military strength but also his innovative tactics, such as attaching sails to cannons for easier transport across the challenging desert terrain of North Africa.

In 1517, the brothers' maritime raids continued unabated. They struck Capo Limiti and later assaulted the town of Isola di Capo Rizzuto in Calabria. These raids were not just acts of piracy; they were strategic moves to disrupt the maritime trade and influence of their adversaries in the Mediterranean.

Oruç Reis's ambitions were not limited to the Mediterranean coast. He extended his conquests to the eastern lands of Morocco. In 1518, he displayed his strategic acumen by conquering and fortifying Oujda and Tibda. He also exerted his influence over the local tribes, such as the Beni Amer and Beni Snassen, imposing tributes upon them and thereby consolidating his power in the region.

Recognizing the threat and potential opportunity presented by Oruç's advances, the sultan of Morocco entered into negotiations with him. These talks culminated in an alliance, a move likely motivated by the sultan's apprehension over the rapid expansion of the Turks under Oruç's leadership. This alliance not only solidified Oruç's position in the region but also marked him as a significant political and military figure whose influence extended beyond piracy and naval warfare to the broader geopolitical stage of North Africa and the Mediterranean.

The conflict between Oruç Reis and the Spanish forces escalated further in 1518, leading to a series of events that would cement Oruç's legacy in the annals of Mediterranean history. The Spaniards, in their bid to control the region, appointed Abu Zayan as the new ruler of Tlemcen and Oran, instructing him to launch a land assault against Oruç. However, demonstrating his strategic foresight, Oruç anticipated this move and pre-emptively struck Tlemcen. His attack was swift and decisive, resulting in the capture of the city and the execution of Abu Zayan during the Fall of Tlemcen in 1518. This victory was significant but came with a notable consequence: Sheikh Buhammud, the sole survivor of Abu Zayan's dynasty, fled to Oran and sought assistance from Spain.

In response, Emperor Charles V personally arrived in Oran in May 1518. He was received by Sheikh Buhammud and the Spanish governor of the city, Diego de Córdoba, Marquess of Comares. The Spanish forces, numbering 10,000 soldiers and bolstered by thousands of Bedouins, prepared for a substantial offensive against Oruç. Meanwhile, Oruç and his brother Ishak fortified their position in Tlemcen with 1,500 levents (elite Ottoman infantry) and 5,000 Moorish soldiers, ready to defend their newly acquired territory.

The ensuing siege was a testament to Oruç's resilience and tactical ingenuity. For six months, he valiantly defended his lands against the combined forces of the Tlemcen emir and the Spanish. However, the situation took a dire turn when Oruç was betrayed by some of the local inhabitants. Faced with overwhelming odds and seeking to break the enemy siege to return to Algiers, Oruç made a daring attempt to cross a river with his remaining levents.

This final stand was both heroic and tragic. Oruç, already known for his bravery and having lost an arm in previous battles, plunged back into the fray, refusing to abandon his levents. However, in the intense battle that ensued while trying to cross the river, most of his levents were killed. Oruç himself, seeing his last levent fall, sustained a fatal spear wound.

The Spaniards, determined to provide evidence of Oruç's death to the King of Spain, severed his head and preserved it in a bag full of honey, a method used to prevent decomposition during transportation. This gruesome act was borne out of the Spaniards' repeated encounters with Oruç, during which they had several times falsely claimed to have killed him.

With Oruç's death, his brother Hızır (later known as Hayreddin Barbarossa) inherited not only his brother's position but also his name (Barbarossa) and his mission. Hızır would go on to become one of the most powerful and renowned Ottoman admirals, securing Ottoman dominance over the Mediterranean Sea during the 16th century. His achievements not only honored the legacy of his brother Oruç but also significantly shaped the course of naval history in the Mediterranean.

Hayreddin Barbarossa

Hayreddin Barbarossa, a legendary figure of the seas, whose original name was Khiḍr and also known as Hayreddin Pasha, Hızır Hayrettin Pasha, or simply Hızır Reis, was born between 1466 and 1483 on the island of Lesbos. His life reads like an adventure novel: from humble beginnings to becoming the feared and respected admiral of the Ottoman Navy, dominating the Mediterranean in the mid-16th century.

His journey began under the tutelage of his elder brother, Oruç Reis, as a corsair. The siblings' daring escapades led them to capture Algiers from Spain in 1516, with Oruç proclaiming himself Sultan. Tragically, Oruç's death in 1518 passed the mantle to Khizr, along with the fearsome nickname "Barbarossa" ("Redbeard" in Italian).

But Khizr was more than a fearsome pirate; he was a strategist. In 1529, he snatched the Peñón of Algiers from the Spaniards, marking a significant shift in power. His career skyrocketed when Suleiman the Magnificent appointed him as Kapudan Pasha (grand admiral) in 1533. This role saw him embarking on diplomatic missions, like his embassy to France, conquering Tunis in 1534, and delivering a crushing defeat to the Holy League at Preveza in 1538. His alliances with the French in the 1540s are tales of cunning and bravery.

Hayreddin Barbarossa's roots were as diverse as his life was extraordinary. Born to an Ottoman sipahi father of Turkish or Albanian descent and a Greek Orthodox mother, he grew up in a multicultural household. His father, Yakup

Ağa, was a respected potter and a savvy businessman who participated in the Ottoman conquest of Lesbos and was rewarded with the fief of Bonova.

The saga of the four brothers, all seasoned seamen, is a captivating tale of adventure and resilience on the high seas. Initially, they embarked on their maritime journey as sailors, but soon, the call of the sea led them to a life of privateering in the Mediterranean, countering the Knights Hospitaller based on Rhodes.

Oruç, the trailblazer, was the first to plunge into seamanship, followed closely by his brother Ilyas. Khizr, not to be left behind, soon captained his own ship, while Ishak managed the financial aspects of their growing marine enterprise.

Their lives at sea were not just about navigating waves; they were multilingual and culturally savvy, with Oruç mastering languages like Italian, Spanish, French, Greek, and Arabic. Tragedy struck during a voyage to Tripoli, Lebanon, when the Knights of St John attacked them, leading to Ilyas's death and Oruç's capture. Held prisoner in Bodrum Castle for nearly three years, Oruç's fate changed when Khizr orchestrated a daring escape.

Their exploits continued to grow in scale and impact. In Antalya, Oruç received 18 galleys from Şehzade Korkut, an Ottoman prince, to combat the Knights, who were disrupting Ottoman trade. Later, with a larger fleet of 24 galleys, Oruç participated in an Ottoman naval mission in Italy, demonstrating his prowess by bombarding coastal castles and capturing ships.

But the tides of fortune are ever-changing. Learning of Korkut's flight to Egypt amid succession disputes, and fearing repercussions due to his association with the exiled prince, Oruç set sail for Egypt. There, he met Korkut in Cairo and even won favor with the Mamluk Sultan Qansuh al-Ghawri, who entrusted him with a ship and a mission to raid Christian-controlled coasts and islands in the Mediterranean.

As winter faded, Oruç, now a formidable force on the seas, left Alexandria, raiding along the coasts of Liguria and Sicily, etching his name into the annals of maritime history as a fearless privateer and a master of the Mediterranean.

In 1503, Oruç's maritime prowess grew as he seized three ships and made Djerba Island his new stronghold, shifting his focus to the Western Mediterranean. It wasn't long before Khizr joined him at Djerba, strengthening their brotherly alliance. The following year, the duo approached Abu Abdallah Muhammad IV al-Mutawakkil, the ruler of Tunis, seeking access to the port of La Goulette, a strategic location for their operations. They struck a deal, agreeing to share a third of their plunder with the sultan.

Oruç, a master at sea, skillfully commandeered small galiots to capture two larger papal galleys near Elba. The brothers' audacity didn't stop there; they soon seized a formidable Sicilian warship, the Cavalleria, along with its crew of Spanish soldiers and knights, off the coast of Lipari. Their exploits continued along the shores of Calabria in 1505, elevating their reputation in the maritime world. This fame attracted other renowned Muslim corsairs, including Kurtoğlu, known in the West as Curtogoli. By 1508, their daring raids extended to Liguria, particularly Diano Marina.

Ishak, the eldest brother, left Mytilene in 1509 to join his siblings at La Goulette. Oruç's reputation soared as he embarked on a noble mission between 1504 and 1510, transporting Muslim Mudéjars from Christian Spain to North Africa. This compassionate act earned him the affectionate title Baba Oruç (Father Oruç), which, through linguistic evolution, became Barbarossa (Redbeard in Italian) in Spain, France, and Italy.

In 1510, the brothers' maritime campaigns intensified. They raided Capo Passero in Sicily, fended off Spanish assaults on Bougie, Oran, and Algiers, and even ventured to Reggio Calabria in Italy. A battle in Bougie in 1512 cost Oruç his left arm, earning him the nickname Gümüş Kol (Silver Arm in Turkish) after he began using a silver prosthetic.

That same year, their audacious raids reached Andalusia, capturing a Genoese galliot and storming through Menorca, Liguria, and Genoa, capturing a fleet of Genoese galleys. After a triumphant spree of seizing 23 ships, the brothers returned to La Goulette, further bolstering their naval strength with more galliots and a gunpowder facility.

The year 1513 saw them raiding Valencia, capturing ships, and clashing with the Spanish fleet. They then moved their base to Cherchell, east of Algiers. In 1514, they decimated two Spanish fortresses at Bougie and repelled a Spanish reinforcement fleet, leading raids against Ceuta and capturing Jijel in Algeria. Their conquests continued across the Mediterranean, including Mahdiya in Tunisia and coasts of Sicily, Sardinia, and Spain.

In 1515, their relentless campaign continued with the capture of galleons and galleys at Majorca. Oruç's tribute to the Ottoman Sultan Selim I was reciprocated with splendid gifts, bolstering their fleet. Joined by Kurtoğlu, they besieged the Castle of Elba, returning to Liguria to capture a dozen ships, cementing their legacy as formidable forces of the Mediterranean seas.

In a pivotal year of 1516, the brothers orchestrated a significant victory by capturing Jijel and Algiers from Spanish control, effectively taking over the governance of the city and its region. This led Abu Hamo Musa III of the Beni Ziyad dynasty to flee. Despite efforts by the local Spaniards in Algiers, who sought help from Charles V, King of Spain and Holy Roman Emperor, and took refuge on the island of Peñón, the Spanish fleet failed to dislodge the brothers from their new stronghold.

Oruç, understanding the strategic advantage of aligning with a powerful ally against Spain, decided to join the Ottoman Empire. In a move to strengthen ties and gain support, he relinquished his title as Sultan of Algiers in 1517, offering the city to Ottoman Sultan Selim I. The Sultan welcomed this move, incorporating Algiers as an Ottoman province and appointing Oruç as its Governor and Chief Sea Governor of the Western Mediterranean, promising support with Janissaries, galleys, and cannon.

The Spaniards, attempting to counteract, appointed Abu Zayan as ruler of Tlemcen and Oran and ordered him to attack Oruç. However, Oruç, learning of this plan, pre-emptively struck Tlemcen, capturing the city and ending Abu Zayan's rule. Sheikh Buhammud, the sole survivor of Abu Zayan's line, fled to Oran and sought Spanish help.

Oruç then set his sights on expanding his territory inland, capturing Miliana, Medea, and Ténès. He innovated by attaching sails to cannons for easier transport through North Africa's deserts. In 1517, they also raided Capo Limiti and later Capo Rizzuto in Calabria.

In May 1518, Emperor Charles V reached Oran, where he was met by Sheikh Buhammud and the Spanish governor, Diego de Córdoba. The Spaniards, bolstered by local Bedouins, marched towards Tlemcen. Oruç and Ishak, defending with a force of Turkish and Moorish soldiers, valiantly held out for 20 days but ultimately fell in battle to Garcia de Tineo's forces.

Following the loss of his elder brother and sensing vulnerability, Khayr al-Din reached out to Selim I in 1519, pledging allegiance and securing Ottoman support. Granted the title of Beylerbey, along with military reinforcements, he not only inherited his brother's position and mission but also his famed name, Barbarossa.

Reinforced by Turkish soldiers from the Ottoman Sultan, Barbarossa swiftly reclaimed Tlemcen in December 1518. He intensified his mission to relocate mudéjars from Spain to North Africa, earning the loyalty of these Muslims who deeply resented Spain. His conquests expanded with the capture of Bône, and in 1519, he successfully repelled a Spanish-Italian army trying to retake Algiers. That same year, he showcased his naval dominance by sinking a Spanish ship and capturing eight others, and even raided regions as far as Provence, Toulon, and the Îles d'Hyères in southern France.

In 1521, Barbarossa's reach extended to the Balearic Islands, and he intercepted several Spanish ships coming from the New World near Cádiz. The following year, he sent his fleet, commanded by Kurtoğlu, to join the Ottoman siege of Rhodes, leading to the Knights of St John's departure from the island in early 1523.

Barbarossa's relentless campaigns continued unabated. In June 1525, he raided Sardinian coasts, and in May 1526, he landed in Crotone, Calabria, sacking the city and destroying Spanish vessels. His naval prowess was on full display as he raided various Italian locations, including Cape Spartivento and Messina, and narrowly avoided confrontation with Andrea Doria's fleet and the Knights of St John off the Tuscan coast.

In 1527, Barbarossa's raids spanned across numerous Italian and Spanish ports and castles. His significant achievement came in May 1529 when he captured the Spanish fort on the island of Peñón of Algiers. He then assisted in transporting 70,000 mudéjars to Algiers, facilitating their safe passage across the Strait of Gibraltar.

Barbarossa's series of raids continued through 1530, targeting Sicily, the Balearic Islands, and various regions along the Mediterranean coasts of Italy and France. In December 1530, he seized the Castle of Cabrera in the Balearic Islands, establishing it as a strategic base for his operations.

The year 1531 saw Barbarossa face off against Andrea Doria, appointed by Charles V to reclaim Jijel and Peñón of Algiers. Barbarossa successfully repulsed the Spanish-Genoese fleet of 40 galleys. He also raided the island of Favignana, where he overcame an attack by the Maltese Knights. Continuing his campaign across Calabria, Apulia, and even Tripoli, he relentlessly harassed the Knights of St John, showcasing his naval supremacy and strategic acumen. His operations in 1531 culminated with further raids along the Spanish coasts and the Îles d'Hyères.

In 1532, as Suleiman I focused on his campaign against Habsburg Austria, Andrea Doria capitalized on this opportunity to seize Coron, Patras, and Lepanto along the Morea (Peloponnese) coasts. This prompted Suleiman to reinforce his naval power. He called upon Barbarossa, who set sail in August 1532 after raiding locations like Sardinia, Corsica, and various islands, and capturing 18 galleys near Messina.

Barbarossa, en route to Istanbul, launched raids along the Calabrian coasts and headed towards Preveza, where he engaged and overpowered Doria's forces, capturing seven galleys. He reached Preveza with a formidable fleet of 44 galleys, later dispatching 25 back to Algiers and proceeding to Constantinople with 19. In the Ottoman capital, Sultan Suleiman welcomed him and appointed him as the Grand Admiral of the Ottoman Navy and Chief Governor of North Africa, granting him governance over the provinces of Rhodes, Euboea, and Chios.

In 1534, Barbarossa left Constantinople with a fleet of 80 galleys. He swiftly recaptured Coron, Patras, and Lepanto from the Spanish, followed by a successful raid across the Strait of Messina and along the Calabrian coast, capturing numerous ships and fortresses.

His campaign continued with raids in Campania, including the sacking of Capri and Procida, and bombarding ports in the Gulf of Naples, resulting in the capture of thousands. He then advanced to Lazio, shelling Gaeta and landing in several coastal towns, even causing alarm in Rome. His forces captured a significant number of captives in Sperlonga and ransacked the palace of Giulia Gonzaga in Fondi. His path of destruction included Vallecorsa, Ponza, Sicily, and Sardinia.

Barbarossa's most significant achievement that year was capturing Tunis and La Goulette, ousting the Hafsid Sultan Mulay Hassan. Charles V's attempt to sway or assassinate Barbarossa spectacularly failed, with the latter executing the emperor's envoy.

However, Mulei Hassan sought Charles V's assistance to reclaim his kingdom. In 1535, a large Spanish-Italian force recaptured Tunis, Bône, and Mahdiya. Anticipating the invasion, Barbarossa had already vacated Tunis, moving to the Tyrrhenian Sea to bombard ports and rebuild a fort in Capri, later named after him. He then returned to Algiers, from where he continued his coastal raids against Spain and the Balearic Islands, capturing several galleys and freeing Muslim oar slaves. In September 1535, he successfully repelled another Spanish attempt to take Tlemcen.

In 1536, Barbarossa was summoned to Constantinople to lead a formidable fleet of 200 ships in an assault on the Habsburg Kingdom of Naples. By July 1537, his campaign was in full swing as he successfully captured Otranto, Castro, and Ugento in Apulia.

That same year, Barbarossa, alongside Lütfi Pasha, spearheaded a major Ottoman offensive against the Venetian territories in the Aegean and Ionian Seas. The islands of Syros, Aegina, Ios, Paros, Tinos, Karpathos, Kasos, Kythira, and Naxos fell to their forces. Barbarossa also launched a raid on Corfu, devastating its agricultural lands and enslaving many of its rural inhabitants. Despite a fierce assault, the Old Fortress of Corfu, strongly defended by the Venetians, resisted his siege. This setback led him to redirect his efforts towards Calabria. Venice, alarmed by these losses, urged Pope Paul III to form a "Holy League" against the Ottoman threat.

In 1538, under Pope Paul III's initiative, a Holy League comprising the Papacy, Spain, the Holy Roman Empire, Venice, and the Maltese Knights was formed to confront the Ottomans. However, Barbarossa, with Sinan Reis, decisively defeated the League's fleet, commanded by Andrea Doria, at the Battle of Preveza in September 1538. This triumph cemented Ottoman naval supremacy in the Mediterranean for over three decades.

Barbarossa's relentless campaign continued into 1539, capturing Skiathos, Skyros, Andros, and Serifos. He reclaimed Castelnuovo from the Spanish and took the Castle of Risan. Alongside Sinan Reis, he attacked the Venetian stronghold at Cattaro and the Spanish fortress near Pesaro. By 1540, after seizing the remaining Christian territories in the Ionian and Aegean Seas, Venice capitulated, signing a peace treaty with Sultan Suleiman and recognizing Ottoman conquests.

In 1540, Barbarossa led a raid on Gibraltar, capturing significant spoils and prisoners, significantly impacting the local population. Later that year, Emperor Charles V attempted to sway Barbarossa to join the Spanish side, offering him a high-ranking naval position and control over Spain's North African territories, but Barbarossa declined.

The refusal led Charles V to personally lay siege to Algiers in October 1541, aiming to quell the corsair menace. Despite the advice of Andrea Doria and Hernán Cortés against such a campaign during an unfavorable season, Charles proceeded. However, his efforts were thwarted by a severe storm that disrupted the landing and severely damaged the Spanish fleet. Forced to retreat, Charles withdrew his battered forces, marking another failure in curbing Barbarossa's dominance in the Mediterranean.

In 1543, Barbarossa, aligning with France, an Ottoman ally, set sail towards Marseilles with an impressive fleet of 210 ships, including 70 galleys, 40 galliots, and 100 other warships, carrying a combined force of 30,000 Ottoman troops. As he navigated through the Strait of Messina, he encountered Diego Gaetani, the governor of Reggio Calabria. Barbarossa's demand for surrender was met with cannon fire, resulting in the death of three Turkish sailors.

Incensed by this defiance, Barbarossa besieged and captured Reggio Calabria. He then proceeded to raid the coasts of Campania and Lazio. Approaching Rome via the Tiber, he posed a significant threat but refrained from attacking the city due to French intervention. His campaign continued with the siege and capture of Nice on 5 August 1543 in the name of French King Francis I.

Barbarossa's fleet then landed at Antibes and Île Sainte-Marguerite near Cannes, followed by the sacking of San Remo, other Ligurian ports, Monaco, and La Turbie. Upon King Francis' orders, Toulon was evacuated and handed over to Barbarossa, who transformed it into a temporary Ottoman outpost, complete with a mosque and slave market.

In spring 1544, Barbarossa returned to San Remo, raided Borghetto Santo Spirito and Ceriale, and defeated a Spanish-Italian fleet, extending his raids into the Kingdom of Naples. He then sailed to Genoa, threatening to attack unless Turgut Reis, a prominent Ottoman admiral captured by Giannettino Doria in 1540, was released. Andrea Doria, hosting Barbarossa at his palace in Genoa, negotiated Turgut Reis' release for 3,500 gold ducats.

Barbarossa successfully defended southern France from further Spanish incursions but was called back to Istanbul following a truce between Charles V and Suleiman in 1544.

Departing Provence in May 1544, Barbarossa again targeted San Remo and, upon reaching Vado Ligure, received a substantial payment from Genoa to prevent further attacks. In June, he appeared off Elba, demanding the release of Sinan Reis' son, captured and baptized by the Spaniards in Tunis a decade earlier. Following his successful release, Barbarossa captured several Tuscan cities, including Castiglione della Pescaia, Talamone, and Orbetello. In a symbolic act of vengeance, he destroyed the tomb and remains of Bartolomeo Peretti in Grosseto, who had previously burned his father's house in Mytilene in 1543.

Barbarossa continued his relentless campaign by capturing Montiano, occupying Porto Ercole and the Isle of Giglio. He even attempted to besiege Civitavecchia, but the siege was lifted following persuasion from Leone Strozzi, the French envoy.

The Ottoman fleet then directed its might against the coasts of Sardinia, before making a formidable appearance at Ischia in July 1544. There, he captured the city, Forio, and the Isle of Procida, and even threatened Pozzuoli. Giannettino Doria, commanding 30 galleys, was forced to retreat towards Sicily, seeking refuge in Messina. Although adverse winds prevented an assault on Salerno, Barbarossa managed to land at nearby Cape Palinuro.

Continuing his journey through the Strait of Messina, he landed at various locations near Reggio Calabria, including Catona, Fiumara, and Calanna, as well as Cariati and Lipari. At Lipari, after a 15-day bombardment of the citadel which refused to surrender, he successfully captured it.

After these extensive campaigns, Barbarossa returned to Constantinople. In 1545, he embarked on his final naval expeditions, bombarding ports on the Spanish mainland and landing at Majorca and Menorca for the last time, before returning to build a palace on the Bosphorus in what is now the Büyükdere quarter of the Sarıyer district.

Barbarossa retired in Constantinople in 1545, designating his son Hasan Pasha as his successor in Algiers. He spent his final days dictating his memoirs to Muradi Sinan Reis, resulting in the five-volume "Gazavat-ı Hayreddin Paşa" (Conquests of Hayreddin Pasha), now exhibited at the Topkapı Palace and Istanbul University Library.

Barbarossa passed away in 1546 in his palace on the Bosphorus in Büyükdere, Istanbul. His final resting place is a notable mausoleum in the Beşiktaş district, designed by the renowned architect Mimar Sinan. Situated near the place where his fleet once assembled, it stands as a testament to his formidable presence in maritime history. A memorial built in 1944 also stands beside his mausoleum, honoring his legacy.

Pier Gerlofs Donia

Pier Gerlofs Donia, a name etched in the annals of history, lived around 1480 to 28 October 1520. More than just a Frisian farmer, he emerged as a formidable rebel leader and a feared pirate, immortalized in lore and memory. In his native West Frisian tongue, he was revered as Grutte Pier ("Big Pier"), a moniker in the pre-1980 West Frisian spelling penned as Greate Pier. This nickname was not mere whimsy; it was a testament to his extraordinary stature, Herculean strength, and undaunted bravery, traits that have become the stuff of legends.

The life of Grutte Pier is veiled in the mists of time, with much of his story interwoven with folklore and hearsay. However, a description by Pier's contemporary, Petrus Thaborita, sheds light on this enigmatic figure. The 19th-century Dutch historian Conrad Busken Huet, drawing upon Thaborita's account, paints a vivid picture of Grutte Pier. He is described as a veritable giant, possessing the strength of an ox, with a commanding presence accentuated by his dark complexion, broad shoulders, and a long, black beard and moustache. More than his physical attributes, Pier was known for his natural, rough humor. Yet, beneath this rugged exterior lay a man shaped by the harsh tides of fate.

A pivotal moment came in 1515, a year marred by personal tragedy for Pier. The bloody injustice that befell him, marked by the slaughter of his kinsfolk and the ruin of his property, ignited a transformative fire within him. From the ashes of his former life as a farmer, Pier rose as a freedom fighter, a role in which he achieved legendary status. His actions were driven by a deep-seated desire for vengeance and justice, making him a figure both feared and admired. His exploits and battles, often romanticized, have firmly placed him in the pantheon of historical figures whose lives blur the line between fact and fiction.

Pier Gerlofs Donia was born around 1480 in the picturesque village of Kimswerd, located near the city of Harlingen in Wonseradeel, part of what is now known as Friesland in the Netherlands. His birth into the world marked the beginning of a life that would later unfold into a tapestry of legend and lore.

Pier was born into a family of at least four siblings, with his roots deeply entrenched in the local nobility and farming community. His father, Gerlof Piers, and mother, Fokel Sybrants Bonga, came from esteemed backgrounds. Fokel, Pier's mother, was notably the daughter of the distinguished Schieringer nobleman, Sybrant Doytsesz Bonga, who hailed from the eminent Bongastate in Kimswerd. This lineage imbued Pier with a sense of identity and belonging to the land and its people, which would later become pivotal in his life's journey.

The personal life of Pier Gerlofs Donia was marked by his marriage to Rintsje Syrtsema, a union that blessed them with two children: a son named Gerlof and a daughter named Wobbel, both born around 1510. The family dynamics of Pier's life, though often overshadowed by his more public exploits, reveal a man who valued family ties and continuity. His untimely death in 1520 left a void, leading to his mother, in her will dated 1525, appointing Pier's brother Sybren as the guardian of Pier's minor children, ensuring their well-being and continuity of the family lineage.

Pier's life was not just defined by his familial roles but also by his professional undertakings. He and his brother-in-law, Ane Pijbes (who was married to Pier's sister Tijdt Gerlofs), jointly managed the farming estate of Meyllemastate in Kimswerd. This partnership in farming not only highlights Pier's deep connection to his land but also his involvement in the local agricultural community, showcasing a facet of his life often eclipsed by his more notorious activities.

An intriguing aspect of Pier's legacy is his purported relationship with Wijerd Jelckama, often referenced in 18th and 19th-century texts. While Jelckama is frequently described as Pier's nephew, contemporary accounts, such as those by Worp van Thabor, simply refer to him as Weird van Bolsward. This ambiguity has led modern historians like J.J. Kalma to question the familial connection. Further complicating this narrative is the assertion by Brouwer in the Encyclopedia of Friesland, which contends that Jelckama was not, in fact, Pier's nephew, but rather his lieutenant, a role that underscores the military and strategic dimensions of Pier's life.

About 7 kilometers northeast of his village of Kimswerd, in the historic city of Franeker, lay the epicenter of a significant military presence that would dramatically alter the course of Donia's life. It was here that the Black Band, a notorious regiment of Landsknechts in the service of George, Duke of Saxony, was quartered. This regiment, known for its ruthless efficiency, was embroiled in the throes of a civil war that pitted the Vetkopers, who were resistant to Burgundian and later Habsburg rule, against the Schieringers.

The Black Band's reputation was formidable, marked by their propensity for violence and lack of restraint. Known to resort to extreme measures when their pay was delayed or insufficient, they frequently extracted forced payments from the villagers, instilling fear and unrest in the region. It was against this backdrop of military oppression and turmoil that a fateful event occurred on January 29, 1515. The Black Band, in a brutal show of force, plundered Donia's village. In a tragic turn of events, they allegedly raped and murdered Donia's wife, Rintze Syrtsema, and razed both the village church and Donia's estate to the ground. This heinous act served as the catalyst for Donia's transformation from a simple farmer to a vengeful freedom fighter.

Driven by a deep-seated desire for revenge, Donia began a guerrilla war against the Habsburgs. His campaign was not just a personal vendetta but also a broader struggle against oppressive rule. He found an ally in Charles of Egmond, Duke of Guelders (1492–1538), aligning himself with the Duke's resistance against the Habsburg dominance.

Pier's armed band, known as the Arumer Zwarte Hoop (which translates to the "Black Hope" or "heap" of Arum in English), gained notoriety as fierce pirates, primarily targeting Hollanders and Burgundians at sea. Their operations, largely conducted on the Zuider Zee (today known as the 'IJsselmeer'), were marked by the successful capture of numerous English and Dutch ships, bolstering their reputation as a formidable naval force. This period of Pier's life, characterized by naval raids and piracy, was a stark contrast to his earlier, more peaceful existence as a farmer.

Pier Gerlofs Donia's campaign in the early 16th century is a striking illustration of his prowess and strategic acumen, particularly evident in his naval operations on the Zuiderzee. In 1517, Pier's activities reached a peak, employing a technique involving "signal ships" to launch aggressive attacks against vessels navigating the waters near the West Frisian coast. His operations were not just limited to piracy; he also played a critical role in transporting Geldrian forces across these waters, deploying them strategically at Medemblik, a location of particular significance in his narrative.

Pier's animosity towards Medemblik and its inhabitants had deep historical roots. This enmity was largely fueled by the town's previous cooperation with the Holland army, commanded by Duke Charles, who would later become Emperor. This collaboration was a sore point for Pier, as it was representative of the larger political and military conflicts that plagued the region. The historical context of Medemblik's involvement in these conflicts dates back to March 1498, when representatives of the Schieringers sought protection from the Vetkopers by aligning with Duke Albrecht of Saxony. This pivotal meeting, which took place in Medemblik, resulted in the Saxon occupation of

Friesland, further complicating the already turbulent political landscape of the Netherlands.

On June 24, 1517, Pier, leading his formidable Arumer Zwarte Hoop, a force comprising approximately 4,000 soldiers from both Frisia and Guelders, embarked on a significant expedition. They sailed towards West Frisia, bypassing Enkhuizen and eventually landing near Wervershoof. From there, they advanced on Medemblik with determination and ferocity. The town, unprepared for such an assault, fell swiftly to Pier and his men. The ensuing carnage saw many of Medemblik's inhabitants either killed or taken prisoner, with the latter group subjected to high ransoms for their release. Some residents managed to escape the onslaught, finding refuge in the relative safety of Kasteel Radboud.

Kasteel Radboud's governor, Joost van Buren, displayed remarkable resilience and tactical skill in the face of this siege, managing to keep Pier's forces at bay. However, the castle's resistance did little to prevent the widespread devastation outside its walls. Unable to breach the castle's defenses, Pier's Arumer Zwarte Hoop vented their frustration by plundering Medemblik and then setting it ablaze. The predominantly wooden architecture of the town offered little resistance to the flames, leading to the near-total destruction of the town, including its church, monastery, and town hall.

The destruction in Medemblik was just one part of a broader campaign of devastation waged by Pier and his army. Following their partial victory there, they continued their relentless march, storming the castles of Nieuwburg and Middleburg near Alkmaar. These fortresses, like Medemblik, were not spared from Pier's wrath. Both were plundered and subsequently set on fire, leaving behind nothing but ruins. These acts of aggression and destruction were emblematic of the turbulent times and the fierce determination of Pier Gerlofs Donia and his Arumer Zwarte Hoop.

The year 1517 marked a particularly aggressive phase in the campaign of the

Arumer Zwarte Hoop, led by Pier Gerlofs Donia. During this period, they captured the town of Asperen, executing a ruthless and comprehensive assault that resulted in the slaughter of almost all its inhabitants. The fortified city of Asperen then served as a strategic base for the Arumer Zwarte Hoop, a testament to their growing influence and control in the region. However, this occupation was short-lived, as they were eventually driven out by the Stadhouder (governor) of Holland, reflecting the ongoing struggle for power and control in the region.

In response to these aggressive actions, including the attacks on Medemblik and Alkmaar, and the perceived failure of the Captain General of Amstelland, Waterland, and Gooiland to adequately defend his territories, a significant countermove was made. The Stadhouder of Holland, recognizing the growing threat, agreed to outfit a formidable war fleet in July 1517. This fleet was placed under the command of Anthonius van den Houte, Lord of Vleteren. Bearing the title "Admiral of the Zuiderzee," van den Houte was tasked with a daunting mission: to rid the region of the Frisian and Gelder piracy that had been disrupting trade and security. Acting on behalf of Charles V, van den Houte embarked on a campaign to reassert control over the troubled waters.

Van den Houte's initial efforts bore fruit, with some of the Frisian vessels being destroyed near Bunschoten. However, this success was met with a fierce counterattack by Grutte Pier, who, in 1518, seized 11 of Holland's ships in a dramatic battle off the coast near Hoorn. This victory once again underscored Pier's naval prowess and his ability to effectively challenge the powers of the time.

Despite these successes, the broader political and military context was shifting against Pier. Unable to stem the tide of Burgundian and Habsburg influence, Pier, disillusioned by the relentless conflict and perhaps recognizing the limits of his campaign, retired in 1519. Leadership of his forces was then passed to Wijerd Jelckama, a figure who had become closely associated with Pier's operations.

Pier's final days were in stark contrast to his life of warfare and rebellion. He died peacefully in his bed on 28 October 1520, at his residence at Grootzand 12 in the Frisian city of Sneek. His burial took place in the 15th-century Groote Kerk (Great Church, also known as the Martinikerk) in Sneek, a city that had become synonymous with his legacy. His tomb, located on the north side of the church, remains a historical landmark.

Dragut

Dragut, known as Turgut Reis in Turkish (1485 – 23 June 1565), was not just an Ottoman corsair and naval commander, but a legendary figure whose very name echoed as "the Drawn Sword of Islam". His leadership saw the Ottoman Empire's maritime dominance spread like wildfire across North Africa. Celebrated for his unmatched military acumen, Dragut stood as a fearsome figure in the annals of naval history. His reputation was such that he was hailed as "the greatest pirate warrior of all time", a mastermind whose strategies and valor placed him leagues above his contemporaries. To the world, he was "the uncrowned king of the Mediterranean", a title he earned through sheer brilliance and skill. A French admiral once lauded him as a living embodiment of the Mediterranean map, equating his land strategies to those of the finest generals of his era. Even Hayreddin Barbarossa, his mentor, acknowledged Dragut's superiority in both courage and skill.

Beyond his exploits at sea, Dragut's influence extended to prestigious titles and administrative roles. He served as the Admiral and Corsair in the Ottoman Empire's Navy under the rule of Suleiman the Magnificent. His administrative prowess was recognized with appointments as Bey of Algiers and Djerba, Beylerbey of the Mediterranean, and eventually as Bey, and then Pasha, of Tripoli. In Tripoli, his legacy was cemented by monumental constructions that transformed the city into a jewel of the North African Coast, showcasing his multifaceted genius and indomitable spirit.

Born in the small village of Karatoprak, now celebrated as Turgutreis in his honor, near Bodrum on the Aegean coast of Asia Minor, Dragut's early life was shrouded in mystery. His birthplace, nestled at the western tip of the Bodrum peninsula, was either in the quaint Saravalos sub-district or possibly in the scenic Karabağ village. His family background was a tapestry of diverse cultural strands, with some sources suggesting Greek Christian roots, while others point towards Turkish Muslim heritage.

Dragut's journey into legendary status began at the tender age of 12. His exceptional prowess with spears and arrows caught the eye of an Ottoman army commander, marking the beginning of his transformative journey. Under the tutelage of this commander, the young Turgut honed his skills in sailing, gunnery, and siege artillery, laying the foundation for his future as a master naval tactician.

His talents soon led him to Egypt in 1517, where he played a significant role in the Ottoman conquest as a cannoneer. In Cairo, his expertise in artillery flourished further. Following the death of his mentor, Dragut moved to Alexandria, embarking on a maritime career that quickly saw him rise through the ranks due to his cannon firing precision.

Dragut's seafaring journey was marked by rapid ascension. Starting as a brigantine captain with a quarter ownership, he soon became its sole owner. His leadership and naval prowess were further solidified when he captained a galiot, armed with advanced cannons, and made a name for himself in the Eastern Mediterranean, particularly targeting Venetian shipping routes.

In 1520, Dragut's fate intertwined with Hayreddin Barbarossa, under whom he flourished, quickly rising to Chief Lieutenant and commanding 12 naval vessels. His conquests were numerous and impactful, capturing the fortress of Capo Passero in Sicily and disrupting maritime routes between Spain and Italy.

His naval campaigns were a blend of strategic brilliance and bold aggression. Commanding a fleet of fustas and barques, he captured Venetian galleys near Aegina in 1533, and played a key role alongside Barbarossa in pursuing Andrea Doria in the Adriatic Sea, capturing several key fortresses and islands.

In a stunning display of naval prowess, September 1538 saw Turgut Reis, commanding 20 galleys and 10 galiots, play a pivotal role in the Battle of Preveza. He led the center-rear wing of the Ottoman fleet, brilliantly outmaneuvering the Holy League, a formidable Christian alliance comprising the Knights of Malta, the Papal States, Venice, Spain, Naples, and Sicily, under Andrea Doria's command.

Despite being massively outnumbered - the Holy League boasted 302 ships and 60,000 soldiers against the Ottoman's 112 ships and 12,000 soldiers - Dragut's strategic acumen shone through. The Ottomans handed the Christian alliance a crushing defeat. Notably, Dragut, with just two of his galiots, captured the Papal galley commanded by Giambattista Dovizi, a knight and abbot of Bibbiena, taking him and his crew prisoner.

The following year, 1539, was a testament to Dragut's relentless pursuit of Ottoman supremacy at sea. Commanding 36 galleys and galiots, he successfully recaptured Castelnuovo from the Venetians, sinking two and capturing three of their galleys. His campaign continued as he landed on Corfu, capturing the galley of Antonio da Canal and engaging Venetian cavalry forces led by Antonio Calbo in Crete.

That same year marked a pivotal moment in Dragut's career. With Sinan Pasha, the Governor of Djerba, appointed as the Commander-in-Chief of the Ottoman Red Sea Fleet, Dragut was named his successor as the Governor of Djerba.

The onset of 1540 saw Dragut's fearsome reputation grow. He captured several Genoese ships near Santa Margherita Ligure and, commanding a fleet of two galleys and 13 galiots, he sacked the island of Gozo. His raids extended to Pantelleria and the coasts of Sicily and Spain with 25 ships, inflicting such havoc that Charles V ordered Andrea Doria to pursue him with 81 galleys. Dragut's campaign of terror continued in the Tyrrhenian Sea, bombarding the southern Corsican ports, notably Palasca, and capturing the nearby island of Capraia. This relentless campaign solidified Dragut's status as a fearsome and strategic naval commander, feared by his enemies and revered by his allies.

Turgut Reis's adventures continued as he set sail towards Corsica, anchoring at Girolata on the island's western shores. In an unexpected turn during the Battle of Girolata, while his ships were undergoing repairs, Turgut and his crew were ambushed by a coalition led by Giannettino Doria (Andrea Doria's nephew), Giorgio Doria, and Gentile Virginio Orsini. This encounter resulted in Turgut's capture, leading to a grueling four-year stint as a galley slave on Giannettino Doria's ship, followed by imprisonment in Genoa. Despite Barbarossa's attempts to ransom him, these offers were flatly rejected.

The tables turned in 1544 when Barbarossa, returning from France with a fleet of 210 ships commissioned by Sultan Suleiman to support King Francis I against Spain, laid siege to Genoa. This bold move forced the Genoese to enter negotiations for Turgut's release. A meeting at Andrea Doria's palace in Fassolo led to an agreement where Turgut was released in exchange for 3,500 gold ducats.

Reunited with Barbarossa, Turgut received command of a flagship and several other vessels. That same year, he led a successful assault on Bonifacio in Corsica, heavily impacting Genoese interests. His campaign continued with an attack on Gozo, engaging the forces of Knight Giovanni Ximenes and capturing Maltese ships loaded with Sicilian goods. In 1545, Turgut's raids extended to the Sicilian coasts and the Tyrrhenian Sea's ports. In July, he devastated Capraia and attacked Liguria and the Italian Riviera with a fleet of 15 galleys and fustas, sacking towns like Monterosso and Corniglia, and landing at Manarola and Riomaggiore.

His relentless assaults continued into the Gulf of La Spezia, capturing Rapallo, Pegli, and Levanto. In 1546, he turned his attention to Tunisia, seizing Mahdia, Sfax, Sousse, and Al-Munastir, using Mahdia as a base against the Knights of St. John in Malta. Back in Liguria, he captured Laigueglia and Andora, briefly pausing before resuming his campaign along the Italian Riviera and targeting San Lorenzo al Mare and Civezza. He then set his sights again on Malta, laying siege to Gozo.

June 1546 saw Andrea Doria, under Emperor Charles V's orders, tasked with driving Turgut away from Malta. However, the two admirals never clashed, as Turgut had already departed for Toulon in August 1546, giving his men a much-needed rest in the safety of a French port.

Following the death of Barbarossa in July 1546, Turgut Reis ascended to the role of the supreme commander of the Ottoman naval forces in the Mediterranean. In July 1547, seizing an opportune moment when the Kingdom of Naples was embroiled in a revolt against Viceroy Don Pietro of Toledo, Turgut launched an assault on Malta with 23 galleys and galiots. He landed at Marsa Scirocco, the southernmost point of Malta facing Africa, and swiftly advanced towards the Church of Santa Caterina, causing the guards there to flee and abandon their post without warning the locals of the impending attack.

After pillaging Malta, Turgut set his sights on Capo Passero in Sicily, capturing a galley belonging to Giulio Cicala, the Duke Vincenzo Cicala's son. He then moved to the Aeolian Islands, capturing a Maltese trade ship with valuable cargo at Salina Island, followed by attacks in Apulia and Salve. His campaign continued in Calabria and Corsica, where he captured several ships.

In 1548, Suleiman the Magnificent appointed him Beylerbeyi (Chief Governor) of Algeria. That year, he also oversaw the construction of a quadrireme galley at Djerba's naval arsenal, which he began using in 1549. Turgut's relentless campaign included capturing Castellamare di Stabia and nearby Pozzuoli in the Bay of Naples, followed by an assault on Procida. He captured a Spanish galley laden with troops and gold at Capo Miseno and seized the Maltese galley La Caterinetta in the Gulf of Naples, intercepting 70,000 gold ducats intended for fortifying Tripoli under Maltese control.

In May 1549, Turgut led 21 galleys towards Liguria, assaulting Rapallo and resupplying at San Fruttuoso. He then landed at Portofino and San Remo, capturing an Aragonese galley from Barcelona. His journey continued through Corsica and Calabria, where he attacked the city of Palmi.

In February 1550, Turgut's fleet of 36 galleys recaptured Mahdia, Al Munastir, Sousse, and most of Tunisia. In May, he attacked the ports of Sardinia and Spain with six galleys and 14 galiots, and although his attempt to seize Bonifacio in Corsica was unsuccessful, he used Gozo as a stopover for replenishing supplies and gathering intelligence on the Maltese Knights.

In June 1550, as Turgut Reis navigated near Genoa, Andrea Doria and Bailiff Claude de la Sengle from the Maltese Knights launched an attack on Mahdia in Tunisia. Meanwhile, Turgut was engaged in his third assault on Rapallo, followed by raids along the Spanish coast. He then ventured to the Tyrrhenian Sea and, in early July, landed on Sardinia's western shores. Upon his return to Djerba, he discovered the attacks on Mahdia and Tunis. Turgut quickly mustered a force of 4,500 troops and 60 sipahis, marching to aid Mahdia's defenders. Despite his efforts, the mission was unsuccessful, and he retreated to Djerba.

By September 1550, Mahdia fell to the combined Spanish-Sicilian-Maltese forces. Concurrently, Turgut was busy repairing his fleet in Djerba. In October, Andrea Doria's fleet blockaded Djerba's lagoon, trapping Turgut's galleys. Ingeniously, Turgut had his ships dragged overland on greased boardways to the island's other side, escaping to Istanbul and capturing a Genoese and a Sicilian galley en route. Notably, Prince Abu Beker, the Tunisian Sultan's son and Spanish ally, was aboard the Genoese vessel.

Upon reaching Istanbul, under Sultan Suleiman's orders, Turgut mobilized a formidable fleet of 112 galleys and two galleasses, crewed by 12,000 Janissaries. In 1551, alongside Ottoman admiral Sinan Pasha, they set out for the Adriatic Sea, severely damaging Venetian ports and disrupting their shipping.

In May 1551, their campaign shifted to Sicily, bombarding its eastern shores, especially Augusta, in retribution for the Sicilian Viceroy's involvement in Mahdia's destruction. They then attempted to seize Malta, landing approximately 10,000 men at Marsa Muscietto. Despite besieging Birgu and Senglea and assaulting Mdina, they abandoned the siege due to insufficient troops.

The Ottomans then targeted Gozo, bombarding its citadel for days. The Knights' governor, Galatian de Sesse, surrendered, leading to the sacking of the town and the capture of about 5,000 Gozitans. Turgut and Sinan departed from Mġarr ix-Xini, transporting the captives to Tarhuna Wa Msalata in Libya. Their next objective was Tripoli, aiming to secure this strategic port and its surrounding area.

In August 1551, Turgut Reis launched a decisive attack on Tripoli (in modern Libya), which had been under the control of the Knights of St. John since 1530. The fort's commander, Gaspare de Villers, along with several knights of Spanish and French descent, were captured during this operation.

However, the French knights were subsequently released following the intervention of Gabriel d'Aramon, the French ambassador in Constantinople. Initially, Ağa Murat was appointed as the governor of Tripoli, but Turgut Reis soon took over the administration himself. In recognition of his significant achievements, Sultan Suleiman bestowed upon Turgut the territory of Tripoli, along with the prestigious title of Sanjak Bey ("Lord of the Standard").

In September 1551, Turgut set his sights on Liguria, capturing the city of Taggia and other ports along the Italian Riviera after Ottoman forces landed at Riva Trigoso. Later that year, he returned to Tripoli, ambitiously expanding his control to include Misrata, Zuwara, Djerba to the west, and extending inland up to Gebel.

In 1552, Sultan Suleiman elevated Turgut Reis to the position of commander-in-chief of the Ottoman fleet, which was dispatched to Italy as part of a treaty between the Sultan and King Henry II of France. Turgut's campaign began with landings at Augusta and Licata in Sicily, followed by the capture of Pantelleria island and castle. In July, he landed at Taormina and neutralized the ports in the Gulf of Policastro. He then took Palmi and advanced towards the Gulf of Naples to rendezvous with another branch of the Ottoman fleet under Sinan Pasha and the French fleet under Polin de la Garde.

Meeting at Scauri, near Formia, Turgut joined forces with Sinan Pasha, but their French ally failed to arrive on time. After a waiting period, Sinan Pasha, obeying Sultan Suleiman's orders, prepared to return to Constantinople. Turgut, however, persuaded Sinan to join him, and together, their fleets bombarded ports in Sardinia and Corsica before successfully capturing the island of Ponza.

The Turkish fleet, under Turgut Reis and Sinan Pasha, initially attacked ports in Lazio belonging to the Papal States and the Kingdom of Naples, despite assurances to the Pope from Henry II. Bad weather redirected them to Massa Lubrense and Sorrento, which they captured, along with Pozzuoli and other coastal areas up to Minturno and Nola.

Andrea Doria of Genoa, in response, led 40 galleys towards Naples. In their first encounter, Turgut Reis captured seven of Doria's galleys. The fleets moved south, culminating in Turgut Reis' victory over Doria at the Battle of Ponza on 5 August 1552.

Suleiman subsequently named Turgut Beylerbeyi of the Mediterranean. Turgut Reis then embarked on extensive campaigns: capturing Crotone,

Castello, and parts of Sicily; attacking Sardinia, Elba, and Corsica; and aiding France by seizing Bonifacio and Bastia. He made various other conquests across the Mediterranean, including the sacking of Vieste, bombarding Ragusa, and raiding Tuscany.

In 1555, Turgut Reis continued his exploits in Calabria, Tuscany, Corsica, Sardinia, and Liguria, capturing and sacking numerous cities and taking thousands of prisoners, showcasing his dominance in the Mediterranean during this period.

In March 1556, Turgut Reis assumed the role of Pasha of Tripoli, where he enhanced the city's fortifications, including the construction of the Dar el Barud (a gunpowder bastion) and the Turgut Fortress, replacing the old Fortress of San Pietro. That July, he captured a Venetian ship near Lampedusa, loaded with supplies for Malta's defense. He also seized Bergeggi and San Lorenzo in Liguria and, by December, had taken Gafsa in Tunisia.

In the summer of 1557, Turgut sailed from the Bosphorus with 60 galleys, attacking Calabria and capturing Cariati, followed by landings in Apulia. The following year, he expanded his territory to include Gharyan, south of Tripoli, and annexed lands from the Beni Oulid dynasty into the Ottoman Empire. His conquests continued with the capture of Taorga, Misrata, Tagiora, and the recapture of Djerba.

Joining forces with Piyale Pasha in June 1558 at the Strait of Messina, they seized Reggio Calabria. Turgut then took control of several Aeolian Islands, landed at Amalfi, and captured Massa Lubrense, Cantone, Sorrento, and areas around Torre del Greco and Tuscany. In August, he seized several ships near Malta and, in September, joined Piyale Pasha in attacking Spanish coasts and capturing Ciutadella in Menorca.

In 1559, Turgut repelled a Spanish assault on Algiers, quelled a revolt in Tripoli, and captured a Maltese ship near Messina. Learning of an impending attack on Tripoli, he returned to bolster the city's defenses, showcasing his strategic prowess and territorial expansion during this period.

Dragut, having antagonized various semi-autonomous rulers around Tunis, faced an alliance in 1560 between them and Viceroy Cerda of Sicily, acting on King Philip II of Spain's orders to capture Tripoli. However, the Ottoman fleet, commanded by Piyale Pasha and Turgut Reis, consisting of 86 ships, decisively defeated Philip II's 200-ship Christian alliance at the Battle of Djerba.

In March 1561, Turgut Reis and Uluç Ali Reis captured Vincenzo Cicala and Luigi Osorio near Marettimo. By June, Turgut landed on Stromboli, and in July, he seized seven Maltese galleys, releasing their commander, knight Guimarens, for a ransom. After resupplying at Gozo, he returned to Tripoli, and in August, he besieged Naples with 35 galleys.

In April 1562, Turgut sent scouts to Malta and laid siege to Spanish-controlled Oran. The following year, he attacked the Granada coast, capturing Almuñécar and 4,000 prisoners, and assisted Salih Reis' siege of Oran with 20 galleys.

In September 1563, Dragut seized six ships near Capri, then captured Naples' Chiaia district. His raids extended to Liguria, Sardinia, and Apulia's Adriatic coast, twice landing at San Giovanni near Messina with 28 galleys. In October, he moved to Capo Passero in Sicily and again clashed with knights on Gozo. His campaigns during these years highlighted his naval prowess and the strategic threat he posed to his adversaries.

During the Great Siege of Malta in 1565, commanded by Sultan Suleiman, Dragut arrived with significant reinforcements, bringing 1,600 to 3,000 men and 13 to 17 ships, landing at Marsa Muscietto on 31 May. This location later became known as 'Dragut Point'. He joined forces with Kızılahmedli Mustafa Pasha, the Ottoman army's commander, who was then besieging Fort St. Elmo.

Dragut recommended capturing Cittadella and Mdina, which were less forti-fied, but his suggestion was ignored. He focused on Fort St. Elmo, controlling the Grand Harbour's entrance, and intensified the bombardment with 30 of his cannons, contributing to the massive 6,000 cannon shots fired in 24 hours. He aimed to isolate Fort St. Elmo from Fort St. Angelo, the Knights' main stronghold.

On 18 June 1565, Dragut was critically injured by a cannonball, though it's unclear if it was enemy fire or an accident. He died from his wounds on 23 June. Historians like Francisco Balbi di Correggio noted his forces' subsequent defeat in Malta, with many believing that his death significantly altered the siege's outcome. The loss of Dragut led to disunity among Ottoman leaders, resulting in strategic missteps that ultimately favored the Knights.

Following his death, Uluç Ali Reis transported Dragut's body to Tripoli, where he was buried in the Sidi Darghut Mosque, still standing and in use today.

Salah Rais

S alah Reis, a figure shrouded in mystery and intrigue, has a birth story that is as enigmatic as his life. He was born either in the bustling port city of Alexandria in Ottoman Egypt or amidst the scenic landscapes of Kazdağ near Çanakkale. His origins are a tapestry of possibilities – he might have been of Turkish, Egyptian, Arab, or even Moorish descent, adding layers of cultural richness to his identity.

From a tender age, Salah Reis was drawn to the adventurous life at sea. He became a part of the crew under the legendary Oruç Reis, also known as Aruj Barbarossa. Oruç Reis, a name that echoed across the West Mediterranean, was renowned as one of the most formidable Ottoman corsairs and privateers hailing from Anatolia. With their base on the Barbary Coast, these seafarers were the scourge of the Western seas, seeking fortune and fame.

In the company of the Barbarossa brothers, Oruç and Hızır Reis, Salah Reis honed his skills in navigation and maritime warfare. He quickly rose through the ranks, showcasing a natural aptitude for leadership and strategy, eventually becoming one of their most trusted lieutenants.

A pivotal moment in Salah Reis' life came when he was about 30 years old. In 1518, Oruç Reis met his end in a fierce battle against Spanish forces in Algeria. This event marked a turning point for Salah, who then aligned himself with Hızır Reis. Hızır, inheriting the formidable title of Barbarossa from his elder brother Baba Oruç (Father Aruj), continued the legacy of their maritime ventures.

In the year 1520, an ambitious expedition took Salah Reis to Djerba alongside Hızır Reis and another notable figure, Turgut Reis. Later that year, they launched a daring assault on Bône, a strategic location under Spanish control. This venture not only demonstrated their naval prowess but also solidified their reputation as fearsome warriors of the sea.

In the year 1529, Salah Rais emerged as a formidable naval commander, leading an impressive fleet of 14 galliots. His first significant operation of that year was a bold assault on the Gulf of Valencia, a strategic maneuver that set the stage for his later exploits. Following this, he joined forces with the fleet of Aydın Reis, participating in the pivotal events of the Turkish-Spanish War near the Isle of Formentera. In this critical battle, the Ottoman forces, showcasing superior naval tactics and ferocity, decisively defeated the Spanish fleet. Tragically, the Spanish commander, Rodrigo Portundo, met his end in this fierce combat.

During the tumult of war, Salah Rais's prowess was further highlighted by his capture of the galley commanded by Captain Tortosa. In a significant turn of events, he also took the son of Admiral Portundo, the Spanish commander, as a prisoner of war, adding a crucial bargaining chip to the Ottoman's strategic assets.

The year 1532 marked another significant chapter in Salah Rais's career. The Ottoman Sultan Suleiman the Magnificent, recognizing the rising tide of Barbarossa's influence and success, summoned him to Constantinople. Salah Rais, now an esteemed officer in Barbarossa's fleet, embarked on this journey in August. The voyage was marked by a series of audacious raids – plundering Sardinia, Bonifacio in Corsica, and the Islands of Montecristo, Elba, and Lampedusa. Near Messina, they achieved a significant victory, capturing 18 galleys. The prisoners from this conquest informed them that Andrea Doria, a Genoese admiral serving Emperor Charles V, was en route to Preveza. Sensing an opportunity, Barbarossa, along with Salah Rais and Murat Reis, swiftly moved to engage Doria's forces. In a short but intense battle, they managed to capture seven of Doria's galleys, forcing the rest to flee.

Barbarossa's fleet, now comprising 44 galleys, made a strategic decision to send 25 back to Algiers, proceeding towards Constantinople with the remaining 19, one of which was under the command of Salah Rais. Upon their arrival, Suleiman the Magnificent received Salah Rais and the other 18 commanders at the Topkapı Palace with great honor. In recognition of Barbarossa's achievements, Suleiman appointed him as Kaptan-ı Derya (Admiral of the Fleet) and Beylerbeyi (Governor General) of North Africa, granting him governance over the Sanjaks (Provinces) of Rhodes, Euboea, and Chios. Salah Rais, in turn, was elevated to the rank of Commodore, a testament to his growing stature and capabilities.

In 1533, Salah Rais and Barbarossa once again joined forces, this time directing their naval expertise against Spanish-controlled ports across the Mediterranean. Their campaigns continued to enhance their reputation as master strategists and fearsome warriors of the sea.

In a significant development in July 1535, Salah Rais was entrusted by Barbarossa Hayreddin Pasha with the critical task of defending Tunis. Accompanied by Cafer Reis and a small contingent of Turkish soldiers, he faced the forces of Girolamo Tuttavilla, Count of Sarno, near the city walls of La Goulette. In a tactical masterstroke, Salah Rais feigned a retreat, luring Tuttavilla's forces into a trap. The ensuing battle saw the fall of Tuttavilla and the capture of his fortress by the Turks. That same month, Salah Rais also assisted Hasan Reis (later known as Hasan Pasha), Barbarossa's son, in governing Algiers.

The year 1536 brought a new assignment for Salah Rais and Barbarossa as they were summoned back to Constantinople to lead the Ottoman naval offensive against the Habsburg Kingdom of Naples. In July 1537, their efforts culminated in the capture of Otranto, along with the Fortress of Castro and the city of

Ugento in Apulia.

August 1537 marked another significant military campaign. Under the leadership of Lütfi Pasha and Barbarossa, a vast Ottoman force, including Salah Rais, embarked on an ambitious operation to capture the Aegean and Ionian islands under Venetian control. They successfully seized Syros, Aegina, Ios, Paros, Tinos, Karpathos, Kasos, and Naxos. Later that year, Barbarossa's forces added another feather to their cap by capturing Corfu from Venice and raiding Calabria once again. These successive victories inflicted considerable losses on Venice, compelling them to appeal to Pope Paul III to form a Holy League against the Ottomans, a move that underscored the significant impact of Salah Rais and his comrades on the geopolitical landscape of the Mediterranean.

In the early months of 1538, Pope Paul III, recognizing the growing threat posed by the Ottoman Empire, successfully rallied a formidable alliance known as the Holy League. This coalition, comprising the Papacy, Spain, the Holy Roman Empire, the Republic of Venice, and the Knights of Malta, represented a significant consolidation of Christian naval power. The leadership of this mighty fleet was entrusted to Andrea Doria, the esteemed chief admiral of Charles V, Holy Roman Emperor. This alliance aimed to curb the expanding influence of the Ottomans in the Mediterranean.

During this period, Salah Rais, who had risen through the ranks to become a Bahriye Sancakbeyi (Rear Admiral, Upper Half), played a pivotal role in the Ottoman naval strategy. In September 1538, he commanded a fleet of 24 galleys, forming the right wing of the Ottoman forces during the critical Battle of Preveza. This battle was a landmark event, where the Ottoman forces, under the command of the legendary Barbarossa Hayreddin Pasha, faced the combined might of the Holy League led by Andrea Doria. Despite their numerical inferiority, the Ottoman fleet achieved a resounding victory, a testament to their superior strategy, leadership, and the prowess of commanders like Salah Rais.

One of the most remarkable episodes of the battle involved Salah Rais and his men in a daring naval engagement. They boarded and fiercely attacked the Galeone di Venezia, the massive Venetian flagship commanded by Alessandro Condalmiero (Bondumier). This assault, carried out alongside attacks on two other Venetian galleys, was particularly notable due to the significant losses the Venetian fleet suffered in oarsmen, a critical factor in naval warfare of the era.

In June 1539, Salah Rais embarked on another significant mission. Setting sail from Constantinople with a fleet of 20 galleys, he joined forces with Barbarossa's fleet near Cape Maleo. This assembly of naval strength was tasked with an ambitious objective – the recapture of Castelnuovo (Herceg Novi) from Venetian control. En route to their primary target, their combined fleet displayed remarkable efficiency and strength, seizing the islands of Skiathos, Skyros, Andros, and Serifos from the Venetians.

In August of the same year, a joint siege was laid on Castelnuovo. The siege, led by the formidable trio of Barbarossa Hayreddin Pasha, Turgut Reis, and Salah Rais, was successful in reclaiming the city. Their campaign of conquest continued as they captured the nearby Castle of Risan, followed by assaults on the Venetian fortress of Cattaro and the Spanish fortress of Santa Veneranda near Pesaro. This relentless campaign effectively weakened the remaining Christian outposts in the Ionian and Aegean Seas.

The culmination of these events led to a significant diplomatic resolution in October 1540. Venice, recognizing the altered balance of power in the region, entered into a peace treaty with Sultan Suleiman the Magnificent. This treaty not only acknowledged the Ottoman territorial acquisitions but also included a substantial payment of 300,000 gold ducats to the Ottoman Empire. This peace treaty marked the end of a crucial chapter in Mediterranean history, with Salah Rais playing a central role in the Ottoman naval victories that reshaped the region's political and territorial dynamics.

The historical narrative of Salah Rais in the 1540s is a tapestry of contested accounts and legendary exploits, illustrating the complex and often conflicting nature of historical sources. According to some Turkish sources, the year 1540 was a tumultuous one for Salah Rais. It is recounted that he, along with the renowned Turgut Reis, found themselves in a precarious situation in Girolata, Corsica. While engaged in the repair of their ships within the harbor, they were reportedly captured by a formidable coalition of Giannettino Doria (the nephew of Andrea Doria), Giorgio Doria, and Gentile Virginio Orsini. These sources paint a vivid picture of the two Ottoman commanders being taken as oar slaves aboard Genoese ships, enduring four years of grueling captivity until their dramatic liberation in 1544. This liberation is attributed to the formidable Barbarossa Hayreddin Pasha, who is said to have issued a stark ultimatum to Genoa, threatening a massive assault with his fleet of 210 ships.

However, this narrative diverges significantly when compared with French, Italian, and Spanish historical accounts. While these sources confirm the capture and subsequent liberation of Turgut Reis, they curiously omit any mention of Salah Rais's captivity. It is hypothesized that the close association and frequent joint operations between Salah Rais and Turgut Reis might have led to some confusion or conflation of their experiences in these records.

In stark contrast to the Turkish sources, French, Italian, and Spanish chronicles place Salah Rais at the forefront of significant military campaigns during this period. Notably, they document his active participation in the Franco-Ottoman conquest of Nice on 5 August 1543, under the command of Barbarossa Hayreddin Pasha. Following this significant victory, Salah Rais is credited with leading a formidable Ottoman force comprising 20 galleys and 3 fustas in a series of assaults along the Costa Brava in Catalonia, Spain. His campaign in Catalonia was marked by a series of aggressive actions, including the sacking of Rosas in early October 1543. The siege and capture of Palamós, following a fierce battle, and the subsequent sacking of San Juan de Palamós, further exemplify his military acumen. His naval prowess is also highlighted in the capture of the Spanish galley Bribona off the coast of Calelh. The cities of

Empúries (Ampurias) and Cadaqués also fell to his forces, culminating in a spree of capturing and sacking, before he set sail for Algiers. Salah Rais's presence alongside Barbarossa in the spring of 1544 further underscores his pivotal role in the Ottoman naval expeditions of that era.

In mid-June 1548, Salah Rais's naval activities continued unabated. He made a notable appearance at Capo Passero in Sicily, commanding a fleet of 18 ships. This expedition was followed by his arrival at Gozo in Malta with 12 ships, having dispatched 6 of his vessels to Algiers to join forces with Turgut Reis, following orders from Hüseyin Çelebi.

An intriguing episode occurred in the autumn of 1550, involving a direct overture from Andrea Doria. Doria, a key adversary and respected figure, attempted to persuade Salah Rais to switch allegiances and serve Spain instead of the Ottoman Empire. This offer, however, was met with refusal.

He joined the fleet of Sinan Pasha and Turgut Reis, playing a pivotal role in a major Ottoman conquest. The target was Tripoli in Libya, a strategic stronghold that had been under the control of the Knights of St. John since 1530, granted to them by Charles V of Spain. Salah Rais distinguished himself in this campaign by effectively bombarding the fortress of the Knights from a mere distance of about 150 steps. His relentless assault eventually compelled Gaspare de Villers, the commander of the Knights, to capitulate and surrender. This triumph in Tripoli not only enhanced Salah Rais's reputation but also led to significant advancements in his career. Upon his return to Constantinople, in recognition of his success, he was promoted to the rank of Bahriye Beylerbeyi (Admiral) of the Ottoman West Mediterranean Fleet. Furthermore, he was appointed Beylerbeyi (equivalent to a Grand Duke) of Algiers in 1551, solidifying his status as a key figure in the Ottoman naval hierarchy.

In April 1552, Salah Rais arrived in Algiers, and from there, he embarked on another naval campaign. Setting his sights on Sicily, he managed to capture a Maltese ship, further demonstrating his naval capabilities. The summer of 1552 saw him joining forces with Turgut Reis in a daring operation in the Gulf of Naples. Together, they launched assaults along the coasts of Lazio and Tuscany, a series of actions that further cemented their reputations as formidable naval commanders. From Italy, Salah Rais ventured to Marseille and then undertook a successful operation against the Island of Majorca (Mallorca), capturing and sacking it.

Following his exploits in Majorca, Salah Rais returned to Algiers. In a strategic shift from naval operations to land-based expansion, he prepared his troops for an overland march into the Sahara Desert. The objective was to extend the boundaries of the Ottoman Vilayet (Province) of Algeria inward. His forces advanced south, capturing the city of Touggourt, strategically situated around an oasis in southern Algeria. Continuing their march, they headed towards Ouargla, only to find it a ghost city, its inhabitants having fled in anticipation of the Ottoman arrival.

The political landscape in Morocco during this time was undergoing significant changes, affecting the dynamics in the region. In 1549, Mohammed ash-Sheikh, the new ruler of Morocco, successfully ousted the Wattasid sultan Ali Abu Hassun, who had declared himself a vassal of the Ottomans and ruled primarily over Fes and its surrounding region. Mohammed ash-Sheikh's conquests included the capture of Tlemcen, ending the Abdelwadid dynasty's rule over the city, and his expansionist policies led him to confront the Ottoman Turks in Algeria.

This Moroccan offensive triggered a swift and robust Ottoman counterattack in 1552, resulting in the recapture of Tlemcen. The Ottomans then advanced towards Fes, where in 1554, they reinstated the Wattasid king Ali Abu Hassun to power. In gratitude, Abu Hassun rewarded the Ottomans with the strategic port of "Badis" on the Mediterranean coast, a site previously captured from the Spanish in 1522. However, this arrangement was short-lived. By September 1554, Mohammed ash-Sheikh had again taken control of Fes, defeating Abu Hassun and his Ottoman allies in the battle of Tadla.

The year 1555 witnessed a significant collaboration between the French Navy, allied with the Ottoman Empire under Suleiman the Magnificent, and Salah Rais, a formidable commander in the Ottoman fleet. This alliance was a strategic move in the larger geopolitical conflict against the Spaniards. The French Navy dispatched a detachment to Algiers, seeking Salah Rais's assistance in their campaign. Demonstrating his commitment to the Franco-Ottoman alliance, Salah Rais agreed to their request and allocated a substantial portion of his naval resources – 22 galleys equipped with Turkish soldiers and cannons – to aid the French fleet.

With the remaining considerable force under his command, estimated at around 40,000 men, Salah Rais then embarked on a significant military campaign. He laid siege to Bougie, a strategic stronghold in the region. The siege was marked by relentless efforts, including a continuous 14-day artillery bombardment. This fierce assault led to the destruction of the city's two primary defensive structures: the Fortress of Vergelette, which controlled access to the port, and the Spanish castle strategically positioned in front of the city walls. Confronted with the overwhelming power of Salah Rais's forces, the Spanish Governor of Bougie, Alfonso di Peralta, chose to negotiate peace rather than continue a seemingly futile defense. The terms of the agreement were remarkably lenient under the circumstances. The surviving Spanish inhabitants were allowed to return safely to Spain with their belongings, and the Spanish forces were permitted to depart with their cannons and weapons. However, the situation took a tragic turn for some of the Spanish civilians. Approximately 400 men, 120 women, and 100 children fell into the hands of local corsairs and were enslaved. Furthermore, upon his arrival in Valencia, Alfonso di Peralta faced a grim fate. He was arrested and subsequently executed on the orders of Charles V for treason, his execution being carried out publicly in Valladolid.

Later in 1555, Salah Rais continued his campaign against Spanish holdings, successfully conquering Peñón de Vélez de la Gomera. Following this victory, he sailed to Constantinople, where he was received with honors by the Sultan, reflecting his growing stature and importance in the Ottoman Empire.

In 1556, Salah Rais embarked on another ambitious military expedition. He set sail from Constantinople towards Oran, a Spanish stronghold in Algeria. Commanding a fleet of 30 galleys, he launched an assault on the city. His forces succeeded in destroying the Spanish forts guarding the port entrance. However, capturing Oran proved to be more challenging than anticipated. The city mounted a fierce defense, bolstered by the local population and the Spanish army garrison, ultimately forcing Salah Rais to withdraw his fleet back to Algiers.

In April 1563, Salah Rais initiated yet another siege on Oran and Mers-el-Kébir, this time with a reinforced military apparatus. He commanded a force of 10,000 soldiers and was joined by Turgut Reis, who provided substantial support with a fleet of 20 ships and 20 pieces of siege artillery. The siege was intense, with Oran once again mounting a determined defense. The city withstood the Ottoman onslaught until it was reinforced by a large Spanish force that arrived in June. Despite not capturing Oran, Salah Rais and his forces succeeded in bombarding and destroying the Fortress of Mers-el-Kébir.

At this stage, a veteran of numerous naval and land campaigns, Salah Rais commanded a substantial force of 15,000 soldiers, playing a crucial role in the Turkish efforts to capture the island, a key stronghold of the Knights of Malta. His strategic acumen was particularly evident in his attack on Fort Saint Michael, a focal point of the Ottoman offensive.

As the siege intensified towards the end of August, Salah Rais demonstrated his tactical prowess by successfully setting up a powerful mine that breached the walls of Castiglia. Capitalizing on this breakthrough, he led an assault force of 4,000 men against the bastion, a move that exemplified his relentless approach to warfare. Concurrently, the main attack on Fort Saint Michael was being commanded by Lala Kara Mustafa Pasha. However, a near-fatal encounter with cannon fire left Mustafa Pasha severely wounded, prompting Salah Rais to step in and assume command of this critical front. He skillfully positioned his troops around the ruins of the Bastion of Castiglia, maintaining the momentum of the siege.

One of the pivotal moments of the siege was the capture of Fort Saint Elmo on the main island. This victory, however, came at a steep cost in terms of casualties. Among the fallen was the legendary Turgut Reis, a lifelong friend and comrade of Salah Rais, who succumbed to his injuries at the venerable age of 80, shortly before the fort's capture. The heavy losses sustained in this operation significantly impacted the Ottoman forces.

Ultimately, the siege was lifted following the arrival of a large Christian fleet assembled to reinforce the Maltese Knights. This timely intervention provided the beleaguered defenders with much-needed support, turning the tide against the Ottoman besiegers.

The Siege of Malta not only marked a turning point in Mediterranean history but also represented the final military mission of Salah Rais. At the time of the siege, he was approximately 77 years old, bringing to close a long and storied career in service to the Ottoman Empire. He passed away three years later, in 1568, in Algiers, closing his life's chapter at a similar age to his friend Turgut Reis.

In a poignant reflection of their enduring legacy, two neighboring town centers in the Province of Manisa in the Aegean Region of Turkey bear their names: Turgutlu and Salihli. These towns stand as a lasting tribute to the remarkable lives and military careers of Turgut Reis and Salah Rais, two figures who left indelible marks on the history of the Ottoman naval expeditions and the broader Mediterranean region.

Yermak Timofeyevich

Yermak Timofeyevich, a renowned Don Cossack warrior, had his origins by the Chusovaya River on the eastern borders of the Muscovite realms. The scant details of his early life are sourced from the Cherepanov Chronicle, a document compiled by a Tobolsk coachman in 1760, well after Yermak's demise. This chronicle, which was never fully published, is believed by historian Aleksandr Alekseyevich Dmitrieyev to be a replication or summary of a genuine 17th-century text. According to its section "On Yermak, and where he was born," Yermak's grandfather, Afonasiy Grigor'yevich Alenin, originally hailed from Suzdal, situated north-east of Moscow.

Afonasiy, seeking to flee poverty, moved to Vladimir in the south. There, he worked as a coachman in the Murom forests, but his life took a turn when he was apprehended for unwittingly aiding robbers as a coachman. Following this, Yermak's father, Timofey, sought better prospects in the Stroganov territories by the Chusovaya River.

Yermak started his career in the Stroganovs' river fleet, handling duties as a porter and sailor, transporting salt along the Kama and Volga rivers. Dissatisfied with this life, he gathered a group of men, abandoned his job, and ventured to the Don region, embracing a life of river piracy. It was here, amidst the Cossack brigands, that he gained the nickname Yermak.

Before his famed conquest of Siberia, Yermak's combat experiences were diverse. He led a Cossack detachment for the Tsar in the Livonian War of 1558–83 and engaged in pirating merchant vessels. As per legends and folk songs, Yermak, alongside the hetman Ivan Kolzo and four other Cossack leaders, spent years robbing and plundering on the Volga. Historian Valerie Kivelson describes Yermak's group as a "gang of thugs." This group, like many Cossacks of the time, was deeply involved in piracy, targeting the Sea of Azov, the Caspian Sea, and various Russian or Persian merchants. Despite his banditry, Yermak established himself as a formidable and loyal Russian combatant, with his military prowess in the Livonian War highlighting his strategic and tactical superiority over other hetmans.

In the late 16th century, the era preceding Yermak's storied expeditions, the Russian state, under the ambitious rule of Ivan the Great, initiated a concerted effort to expand eastward into the vast, uncharted terrains of Siberia. This expansion was primarily motivated by the lucrative fur trade, a resource Siberia was richly endowed with. Initially, the Russians attempted to penetrate northwest Siberia. However, they quickly discovered the formidable challenges posed by this route. As one historical account notes, "to approach Siberia from that direction proved too arduous and difficult, even in the best of times."

Recognizing the need for a more feasible approach, Russian strategists contemplated an alternative southern route. This path would traverse through the Tatar khanate of Kazan, a region pivotal to accessing Siberia's riches. However, for this route to become viable, the Russians first had to overcome a significant obstacle: the conquest of Kazan itself. This task fell to Ivan the Terrible, who, upon ascending to power, made the overthrow of Kazan his foremost foreign objective.

In the early days of October 1552, Ivan the Terrible's modernized army, equipped with cutting-edge military technology and tactics of the time, successfully besieged Kazan. This victory was not just a military triumph but also a strategic one, as it paved the way for Russian expansion into Siberia.

It opened the eastern frontiers to Russian exploration and exploitation, allowing enterprising individuals and families, most notably the Stroganovs, to establish a foothold in the region. Anika Stroganov, seizing this opportunity, used the newly conquered former khanate of Kazan as a gateway into Siberia, eventually establishing a private empire in the southwest corner of the Siberian expanse.

Following the conquest, the Tatar khanate of Kazan was transformed into the Russian province of Perm. Ivan the Terrible, recognizing the entrepreneurial and administrative talents of the Stroganov family, entrusted them with this newly acquired province. He perceived this as a strategic investment, one that would undoubtedly bring future economic benefits to Russia. Furthermore, the tsar granted the Stroganovs the rights to expand into territories along the Tobol and Irtysh Rivers, lands under the dominion of the Muslim leader Kuchum Khan.

The Stroganovs, armed with these permissions, embarked on a series of eastward expeditions into territories that were yet to come under Russian influence. Their endeavors were particularly focused on the khanate of Sibir, a sister state of the former khanate of Kazan. Sibir held significant sway over the western Siberian fur trade, a resource of immense value. This focus on Sibir was strategic, aiming to secure control over these lucrative fur resources, which were pivotal to the economic and territorial expansion of Russia into Siberia.

In the mid-16th century, during the era of Russia's aggressive push towards the East with the conquest of Kazan in the 1540s and 1550s, the khanate of Sibir was embroiled in its own internal strife. Rival clans vied for power, creating a turbulent and unstable political landscape. This precarious situation persisted until the ascension of Kuchum Khan in the 1560s, a formidable leader boasting descent from the illustrious Chingis Khan. Kuchum Khan, recognizing the looming threat posed by the Russian expansion and particularly the Stroganov family's ventures across the Ural Mountains, strategically allied with neighboring states and the Crimean Tatars. His goal was clear: to thwart the Stroganovs' eastward incursions.

In a bold move, Kuchum Khan initiated a raid on Stroganov settlements in July 1572, an attack that tragically resulted in almost a hundred fatalities. The subsequent year witnessed a significant transformation within the Tatar military structure. Leadership of the Tatar army shifted to Kuchum's nephew, Mahmet-kul, marking a new phase in the conflict. The Stroganovs, facing this heightened threat, realized that a purely defensive strategy was insufficient. They needed to take the offensive to secure their interests in the Perm region. Initially, the Tsar granted the Stroganovs permission to launch an invasion into Asia. However, this decision was quickly retracted due to concerns about Russia's capacity to challenge Kuchum Khan's well-entrenched empire, both in terms of resources and manpower.

Defying the Tsar's reversal, the Stroganovs, particularly under the leadership of Anika Stroganov's grandsons, Nikita and Maksim, made a bold decision in the late 1570s. They recruited Cossack fighters, renowned for their military prowess, to lead an offensive against the Tatar forces. Among these recruits, Yermak Timofeyevich emerged as a prominent figure, eventually being chosen as the commander of the Cossack brigades.

The Stroganov Chronicle, a key historical source, records a significant event on April 6, 1579. Moved by tales of Yermak's daring and bravery, the Stroganovs extended an invitation to him and his comrades, calling them to their ancestral estates in Chusovaya to rally against the Tatars under the Tsar's banner. Yermak's reputation as a formidable warrior led to his appointment as the ataman (captain) of the campaign, dubbed the "conquest of Siberia."

However, historical accounts regarding the genesis of Yermak's campaign are not without controversy. A notable discrepancy exists between the narratives presented in the Stroganov Chronicle and another Siberian chronicle, the Yesipov Chronicle. The former depicts the Stroganov family as the primary instigators of Yermak's campaign, while the latter omits any mention of the family's involvement. This discrepancy has fueled debate among historians, with some speculating that the Stroganovs may have crafted their narrative to position themselves alongside Yermak as pivotal figures in the Siberian conquest, thereby bolstering their legacy and influence. The historical community remains divided on this issue, with some scholars attributing significant influence to the Stroganovs in Yermak's campaign, while others argue that they played a minimal role, if any, in its inception.

In the pivotal spring of 1582, Yermak Timofeyevich was formally recruited by the influential Stroganov family for a mission of great significance and challenge. His objective was to assert physical control over the territories along the Tobol and Irtysh rivers, areas which, by virtue of the Tsar's charter of 1574, were already legally under the Stroganovs' domain. The broader strategic aim of this expedition was to forge a southern route to Mangaseya, a region renowned for its rich fur resources. However, the Khanate of Sibir posed a formidable barrier, effectively blocking access from the Ural Mountains to Mangaseya. Yermak's journey, stretching an arduous five thousand miles, was ultimately intended to reach the distant shores of the Bering Strait.

Leading a diverse army of 840 men, Yermak's force included 540 of his own followers and an additional 300 warriors provided by the Stroganovs. This assembly represented a melting pot of nationalities, including Russians, Tatars, Lithuanians, and Germans, with the latter two groups originating from the Lithuanian front. Recognizing the critical nature of their mission, Nikita and Maksim Stroganov invested a substantial twenty thousand rubles from their wealth to equip the army with the finest weapons available at the time. This investment proved particularly advantageous for the Russian contingent, as it provided them with a significant technological edge over their Tatar adversaries, who were primarily equipped with traditional weaponry such as bows, arrows, and spears. In contrast, Yermak's forces boasted matchlock muskets, sabers, pikes, and a number of small cannons, according to Russian history specialist W. Bruce Lincoln. However, there is some historical debate regarding the extent of Yermak's armament. Russian author Yuri Semyonov contends that Yermak's forces had limited access to firearms and no cannons, and were further disadvantaged by a lack of cavalry, in stark contrast to the mobile mounted forces of Kuchum Khan.

Yermak's expedition officially commenced from a frontier fort in Perm, located on the Chusovaya River, on September 1, 1582. Notably, there are differing historical accounts about the exact start date of his campaign, with some sources suggesting it could have been as early as 1579 or as late as 1581. The journey through Siberia was a formidable challenge, navigated with high-sided boats designed in Russia, providing vital protection against attacks from Kuchum Khan's native allies. The absence of horses meant the Cossacks had to carry their supplies on their backs while crossing the Urals, adding to the expedition's hardships.

After a grueling two-month trek across the Urals, following the Tura River, Yermak's forces reached the periphery of Kuchum Khan's empire. Their journey eventually led them to the gates of Qashliq, the khanate's capital. On October 23, 1582, a pivotal battle unfolded at the Chuvash Cape, marking the beginning of three days of intense combat against Kuchum's nephew, Mehmet-kul, and the Tatar forces. Yermak's infantry, leveraging their superior firepower, managed to repel the Tatar charges with volleys of musket fire. This strategic use of firearms inflicted a critical injury on Mahmet-kul and remarkably prevented any Russian casualties. The successful capture of Qashliq by Yermak's army marked a turning point in the campaign, symbolizing the effective "conquest of Siberia" and the culmination of the Stroganovs' ambitious vision.

Yermak's conquest of Qashliq, although a significant victory, came at a steep cost. His Cossack force was drastically reduced to around 500 men, and he was confronted with a severe supply crisis. The city, although rich in treasures like fur, silk, and gold, was devoid of essential food and provisions, as the inhabitants had fled, taking their supplies with them. However, a turn of events occurred four days after Yermak's claim on Qashliq. The local people, including the Ostyak community, returned to the city. Yermak quickly established a rapport with the Ostyaks, who formally pledged their allegiance to him on October 30. This alliance was solidified with offerings of food to the Cossacks, providing much-needed relief.

The Ostyak tributes were crucial in sustaining Yermak's band through the winter. Despite this support, the supplies were insufficient, compelling the Cossacks to venture into the wilderness for fishing and hunting. However, their situation remained precarious. Yermak's victory over the Tatars hadn't eradicated their threat entirely; they continued to harass the Cossacks, impeding Yermak's efforts to gain full control of the region. This persistent threat manifested tragically on December 20, when a group of twenty Cossacks was ambushed and killed by the Tatars. Yermak, upon investigating their disappearance, discovered that Mahmet-kul had recuperated from their previous encounter and was responsible for the attack. Yermak engaged in another battle with Mahmet-kul, emerging victorious once more.

In the following spring of 1583, Mahmet-kul returned, only to be swiftly ambushed and captured by a small detachment of Cossacks, numbering between 10 and 50. Following his capture, Mahmet-kul communicated with Kuchum Khan, urging a halt to attacks on the Cossacks and those paying tribute to Yermak. Seizing this period of reduced hostilities, Yermak proceeded to further his campaign down the Irtysh and Ob rivers, aiming to subdue local tribal leaders. He encountered the Ostyak prince Demian, who had fortified himself with 2,000 fighters in a stronghold on the Irtysh. Demian's fortress, reputedly protected by a gilded idol, posed a significant challenge. Yermak's forces, after an arduous effort, overcame the fortress, only to find no idol within. After dispersing Demian's priests and warriors, Yermak focused on subjugating the most influential local prince, Samar, who had allied with eight other princes. Exploiting Samar's lack of vigilance, Yermak launched a surprise attack, resulting in Samar's death and the dissolution of his forces. This victory allowed Yermak to extract tribute from the remaining princes.

Continuing his journey downriver, Yermak next targeted Nazym, a key Ostyak town. The battle for Nazym was fierce, resulting in the death of Yermak's friend, Ataman Nikita Pan, and several Cossacks. Yermak then directed his campaign along the Ob river, capturing several smaller forts. Upon reaching a point where the river widened significantly, Yermak decided to halt the expansion and returned his forces to Qashliq. This strategic retreat marked a pause in his extensive campaign, allowing him to consolidate his gains and plan for future endeavors in the region.

Upon his strategic retreat to Qashliq, Yermak Timofeyevich was faced with several critical decisions. Among these was the need to communicate his conquests to both the Stroganovs and Tsar Ivan the Terrible. Historians speculate that Yermak's motivations were twofold. Firstly, he sought to rehabilitate his reputation, previously marred by his history of misdeeds. Secondly, and perhaps more urgently, Yermak was in dire need of supplies to sustain his campaign and his men. To accomplish this task, he dispatched his trusted lieutenant Ivan Kolzo along with fifty men. They carried two important letters, one for the Stroganovs and another for the Tsar, as well as a significant quantity of furs intended as a tribute for Ivan the Terrible. The quantity of furs sent has been a matter of historical debate, with estimates ranging from 2,500 to 5,000, and even as specific as sixty sacks.

The timing of Kolzo's arrival at the Stroganov estate was fortuitous. Maksim Stroganov had just received a condemning letter from Ivan the Terrible about Yermak, threatening death upon him and his followers. Kolzo's news of Kuchum's defeat, the capture of Mahmet-kul, and the subjugation of the Tatar lands was therefore greeted with great relief. Maksim Stroganov provided Kolzo with lodging, food, and money, recognizing the importance of his message and mission.

Kolzo's journey then led him to Moscow, where, despite a bounty on his head, he was granted an audience with Tsar Ivan. Ivan, having just concluded the Livonian War and troubled by reports of tribal raids in Perm, was initially in a sour mood. However, the news of Yermak's successes and the expansion of his dominion brought a swift change in his demeanor. Ivan became elated, promptly pardoning the Cossacks and elevating Yermak to the status of a national hero. This jubilation spread throughout Moscow, with church bells ringing in celebration of Yermak's achievements.

Tsar Ivan prepared numerous gifts for Yermak, including his personal fur mantle, a goblet, two suits of armor adorned with bronze double-headed eagles, and a sum of money. Additionally, Ivan ordered that a contingent of streltsy, Russian elite soldiers, be sent to reinforce Yermak's forces. The exact number of these reinforcements is debated, ranging from 300 to 500 men. The Stroganovs were also instructed to supplement this force with an additional fifty men upon their arrival in Perm. Yermak was honored with the title "Prince of Siberia" by the Tsar, who also commanded that Mahmet-kul be brought to Moscow.

Upon Kolzo's return to Qashliq, he relayed the Tsar's orders to Yermak, including the directive to send Mahmet-kul to Moscow. Aware that complying with this order would likely provoke Kuchum and eliminate any remaining chance for peace, Yermak nonetheless proceeded to arrange for Mahmet-kul's transport. As anticipated, this action led to an escalation in Kuchum's attacks.

Meanwhile, Yermak faced another predicament. A harsh winter had hampered efforts to gather supplies and tributes, and the eagerly anticipated reinforcements from the Tsar had not yet arrived. The Stroganovs had indeed contributed fifty cavalrymen to the reinforcement party as instructed by the Tsar, but the challenging Siberian terrain and the burden of the horses had significantly slowed their progress. It wasn't until the spring of 1584 that these reinforcements finally began crossing the Ural Mountains, leaving Yermak and his men in a precarious situation as they awaited much-needed support.

In September of 1583, Yermak Timofeyevich found himself in a precarious situation when he received a plea for help from a Tatar leader named Karacha.

The message conveyed Karacha's request for assistance against the Nogai Tatars, a rival group. Yermak, though skeptical of Karacha's intentions, decided to respond. He dispatched his lieutenant, Ivan Kolzo, along with a contingent of 40 Cossacks to provide the requested aid. However, this decision proved to be a grave miscalculation. Upon their arrival, Kolzo and his men were ambushed and killed in a trap set by Karacha. This loss significantly weakened Yermak's forces, reducing his numbers to just over 300 men.

The tribes that had previously submitted to Yermak's authority sensed his diminishing power and started to revolt. The situation escalated rapidly as Qashliq came under siege by a combined force of Tatars, Voguls, and Ostyaks. The attackers employed a tactical encirclement of the city using a line of wagons, which served dual purposes: it hindered any movement in or out of the city and provided a shield against the Cossacks' firearms. Despite being hampered by limited supplies, Yermak and his men managed to withstand the siege for three months.

In a daring move on the night of June 12, 1584, Yermak orchestrated a surprise attack against the besieging forces. Exploiting the cover of darkness and a cloudy sky, his men stealthily breached the line of wagons and attacked the enemy troops, catching them off-guard in their sleep and inflicting significant casualties. This successful raid not only broke the siege but also allowed Yermak to recover a substantial amount of provisions from the enemy's encampment.

Karacha, having failed in his attempt to defeat Yermak, faced severe repercussions from Kuchum Khan, who executed Karacha's two sons as punishment. Driven by the loss of his sons, Karacha rallied the native tribes for another assault on Yermak the following day. However, this attempt too ended in failure, with Yermak's forces managing to kill a hundred of Karacha's men while suffering only two dozen casualties.

Following this defeat, Karacha retreated to the steppes of the Ishim, where

Kuchum Khan was waiting. Meanwhile, Yermak, no longer confined to defending Qashliq, shifted to an offensive strategy. He embarked on a series of campaigns, conquering numerous towns and forts east of Qashliq and thus further extending the tsar's dominion. Over the summer of 1584, he navigated up the Irtysh River, subduing tribes and demanding tribute. Despite attempts to locate Karacha, Yermak was unable to capture him.

However, Yermak's victories were tempered by significant challenges. His forces were nearly depleted of gunpowder, and the long-awaited reinforcements arrived in a state of utter exhaustion, ravaged by scurvy. Many, including their commanding officer, had perished during the arduous journey. This influx of additional men, far from being a relief, only exacerbated the existing food shortage. Reports from the period suggest that the situation became so desperate that Yermak's men resorted to cannibalism, consuming the bodies of the deceased to survive.

The exact circumstances of Yermak Timofeyevich's demise remain shrouded in the mists of history, with only legends and varying accounts to hint at the final chapter of his life. By the time of his death, Yermak and his men were in the throes of a severe famine, a situation that Kuchum Khan, ever the astute strategist, sought to exploit.

According to the most prevalent version of the story, Kuchum deliberately fed false information to Yermak. The ruse suggested that Bukharan merchants from Central Asia, laden with substantial food supplies, were being blockaded by Kuchum's forces. In August 1584, driven by desperation, Yermak led a group to liberate these traders. However, upon realizing the deception, Yermak ordered a retreat back to Qashliq.

During their return journey, Yermak's party made a critical decision to stop for the night on a small island created by the bifurcation of the Irtysh River. The decision was either due to a raging storm or exhaustion from rowing upstream. On the night of August 4–5, 1584, Yermak's men, confident in the natural protection offered by the river, unwisely chose to sleep without setting a guard.

Unbeknownst to them, Kuchum had been tracking their movements and chose this moment to strike. Taking advantage of the cover provided by the storm and darkness, Kuchum's forces stealthily crossed the river. They launched a surprise attack on Yermak's camp around midnight, catching the Russians completely off guard. The attack was so sudden and fierce that Yermak's men barely had time to reach for their weapons. A brutal massacre ensued, leaving all but three of the Russian side dead, including Yermak.

As legend tells it, Yermak, having fought valiantly and sustained a knife wound to the arm, sought to escape by crossing the river. Tragically, the weight of the armor gifted to him by Tsar Ivan – adorned with a bronze eagle – caused him to sink and drown. A sole survivor, unencumbered by such heavy armor, managed to escape and bring news of Yermak's death back to Qashliq.

In the aftermath, Yermak's body, identified by the eagle on his armor, was discovered seven days later by a Tatar fisherman named Yanish. The Tatars treated Yermak's corpse with a mix of disdain and respect, initially hanging it on a frame for archery practice. However, as time passed, strange phenomena were reported – animals refused to scavenge his body, it produced no odor, and it allegedly caused fear and nightmares among the people. Acknowledging these ominous signs, the Tatars ultimately accorded Yermak a hero's burial. They slaughtered thirty oxen in his honor, and his distinguished armor was distributed among the Tatar chiefs, marking the end of a remarkable and tumultuous life.

Conclusion

As we conclude our journey through the tempestuous and enigmatic seas of pre-1600 piracy, we stand at a crossroads of understanding, not only of the pirates who navigated these waters, but also of the world they helped forge. These seafaring rebels, often merely a footnote in the grand narrative of history, were indeed pivotal in weaving a rich tapestry of conflict, innovation, and intercultural exchange.

The chronicles of these pirates transcend the simple tales of high-seas adventure and looting. They embody the quintessential human yearning for liberty, the courage to explore, and the audacity to challenge authority. These outlaws of the ocean questioned the dominion of empires over the boundless seas, directly confronting the powers of their time.

Their influence was far-reaching and multifaceted. Economically, they were disruptors of trade routes, compelling nations to rethink their maritime strategies and defenses. Politically, they were catalysts for significant shifts in global power structures, exemplified by the Mediterranean dominance of the Barbarossa brothers. In terms of technology, they were innovators in shipbuilding and navigation, pushing the limits of seafaring capabilities. Culturally, they were inadvertent envoys of their age, disseminating a plethora of ideas, technologies, and customs across the oceans.

Nonetheless, the story of these early pirates is not one of mere glorification. Their existence was deeply entrenched in violence, and their deeds often wrought havoc on those they crossed paths with. This dichotomy in their legacy - as figures both admired and abhorred - underscores the intricate tapestry of history and the individuals who shape it.

Reflecting on their lives and times, we recognize that these pirates were a product of their era, shaped by its political, social, and economic currents. They were rebels in an age when maritime rules were nascent, charting not just the physical waters but also the unexplored realms of law, governance, and ethics. Their very existence was a challenge to the prevailing order, prompting empires and monarchies to reassess their maritime dominion.

The waning of this early era of piracy heralded the dawn of new maritime chapters - the age of exploration and the rise of colonial empires. The strategies and lessons gleaned from interactions with these pirates laid the groundwork for future naval tactics and maritime legislation, influencing the course of global trade and international relations.

But the resonance of these pirate stories goes beyond historical impact; they strike a chord with the enduring human spirit - a spirit that craves adventure, cherishes freedom, and straddles the fine line between heroism and villainy.

As we bid farewell to this narrative, we are left to ponder the lasting fascination with pirates. Their allure stems not solely from their bold escapades but from their representation of the human struggle against various forms of constraint. Their defiance epitomizes a raw, unfiltered aspect of the human spirit, an inherent desire to break free from boundaries and venture into the unknown.

The sound of their cannonades has long been silenced, and their ships have vanished beneath the ocean's depths. Nevertheless, the legacy of these pre-1600 pirates perseveres. It endures in our continued intrigue with the ocean's mysteries, in our admiration for those who dare to defy convention, and in our relentless pursuit of freedom and adventure.

As our world evolves, the tales of these early pirates acquire new interpretations, reflecting the contemporary human condition and aspirations. In an era increasingly defined by regulations and norms, the pirate symbolizes unbridled freedom and a challenge to authoritarianism.

Ultimately, the story of these early pirates is more than a relic of the past; it is a narrative that continues to influence our present and shape our future. Their lives stand as a testament to the indomitable human spirit that refuses to be constrained, whether on land or at sea.

Moving forward, let us embrace the lessons gleaned from these maritime shadows. Let's remember the valor in exploring the unknown, the resilience in facing adversity, and the continuous quest for freedom that characterizes not just the pirates of yore but each of us as we navigate the uncharted waters of our existence.

In this way, the essence of these long-forgotten pirates endures, not merely within the pages of history but in the hearts and minds of all who dare to dream and challenge the status quo. The horizon beckons with limitless potential, waiting to be unveiled by those brave enough to embark on the journey.

Bibliography

Baikalov, Anatole V. The Conquest and Colonisation of Siberia. The Slavonic and East European Review.

Bradford, Ernle. The Sultan's Admiral: The life of Barbarossa. London, 2021.

Burgess, Glyn S. Two Medieval Outlaws: Eustace the Monk and Fouke Fitz Waryn. Woodbridge, Suffolk: D S Brewer, 1997.

Curry, Hamilton. Sea-Wolves of the Mediterranean. London, 2014.

Cushway, Graham. Edward III and the War at Sea. Woodbridge, Suffolk: The Boydell Press, 2011.

Duncombe, Laura. Pirate Women: The Princesses, Prostitutes, and Privateers Who Ruled the Seven Seas. Chicago Review Press, 2019.

Dzino, Danijel. Illyricum in Roman Politics, 229 BC–AD 68. Cambridge University Press, 2010.

Fang, Xuanling, editor. Book of Jin (Jin Shu). 648.

Haywood, A. J. Siberia: A Cultural History. Oxford: Oxford University Press.

Livy. History of Rome. Translated by Rev. Canon Roberts, edited by Ernest Rhys, J. M. Dent & Sons, Ltd., 1905.

Lornsen, Boy. Klaus Störtebeker: Gottes Freund und aller Welt Feind. Carlsen Verlag GmbH, 2005.

Ormerod, Henry. Piracy in the Ancient World. Johns Hopkins, 1996.

Polybius. The Histories. Translated by W. R. Paton, F. W. Walbank, Christian Habicht, Harvard University Press, 2010.

Wolf, John. The Barbary Coast: Algeria under the Turks. Norton, 1979.

9 798886 906835 4